Kenneth L. Carder

Who

DOCTRINE, MINISTRY,

Are

AND MISSION

We?

OF THE UNITED METHODIST CHURCH

Leader's Guide

WHO ARE WE?
Doctrine, Ministry,
and Mission of The United
Methodist Church

Leader's Guide
Copyright © 1998 by The United Methodist Publishing House.
Revised edition © 2001.
All rights reserved.

An official resource for The United Methodist Church prepared by The United Methodist Publishing House; 201 Eighth Avenue South, P.O. Box 801; Nashville, TN 37202-0801. Printed in the United States of America.

For permission to reproduce any material in this publication, call-615-749-6422 or write to the Permissions Office; 201 Eighth Avenue, South, P.O. Box 801; Nashville, TN 37202-0801. FAX 615-749-6128.

To order copies of this publication, call 1-800-672-1789.

ISBN: 978-1-4267-7887-2

07 08 09 00 — 10 9 8 7 6 5 4 3

CONTENTS

To the Leader

This is an exciting time to study the statements in *The Book of Discipline of The United Methodist Church* regarding doctrine, ministry, and mission of the denomination. Wrestling in local congregations with these statements will help reclaim our heritage and clarify our understanding about how we should move into the future. This study will help us understand the answer to the question "Who Are We?"

This leader's guide suggests some ways that you and a group of adults in your congregation can wrestle with material prepared by the 2000 General Conference and preceding assemblies.

You may use this material in a variety of settings—a Sunday school class, a weekly weekday study group, a special retreat for church leaders, a series of meetings of the United Methodist Women or the United Methodist Men. You might even use this material in a church membership class.

This leader's guide is organized into thirteen sessions. Each session includes four types of material:

- a statement of purpose and goals:
- discussion of how the new theological statement is grounded in Scripture;
- extended commentary about a portion of the theological statement;
- a session plan with detailed, step-by-step directions.

In most cases, this leader's guide contains more biblical background and commentary on the *Discipline* than is required explicitly by the session plans. You as leader will need to decide how much of that extra material you want to give to group members.

Be sure to read each session plan ahead of time with an eye open for special supplies or other preparations that are required.

The leader's guide is designed so that it can be used by groups or classes meeting for as few as six one-hour sessions (or perhaps for a two-day retreat) or as many as thirteen one-hour sessions. If you are planning for only six sessions, you will probably want to use Sessions 1, 4, 5, 6, 8, and 9. If you plan to gather for thirteen sessions, use all the session plans in the order in which they are printed here. If you expect to meet for more than six sessions but fewer than thirteen sessions, use the basic six sessions plus any others you select in the order in which they are printed in this leader's guide.

Before any of the sessions begin, browse through the annotated list of resources under "For Further Study" (page 113 of this leader's guide) to see which ones might be of use to you as you lead this study. Check with your church librarian and your pastor to see whether some of those items may be borrowed readily and used during class sessions.

This study of doctrine, ministry, and mission of The United Methodist Church will help participants get acquainted (or reacquainted) with our roots and capture a vision of our future.

This study also will enable adults in local churches to learn what theology is and how to do theology in a faithful manner. In the process, this study will help participants say, "That's who I am."

A CHURCH IN SEARCH OF IDENTITY AND MISSION

Purpose of This Session:
To help adults recognize that the primary identity and mission of the church are rooted in God and God's mission to the world.

Goals of This Session:
1. To help study group members recognize that theology is central and necessary to the church's existence and the faithful fulfilling of its mission.
2. To equip adults to identify some key biblical images of the church.
3. To motivate adults to study "Doctrinal Standards and Our Theological Task" and "The Mission and Ministry of the Church" as contained in *The Book of Discipline* (pages 41–94) as resources for understanding the nature and mission of the church.

GROUNDING IN SCRIPTURE

The Bible is the primary source for defining the nature and mission of the church. Attempts to discover the church's identity, formulate its mission, and chart its future must be grounded primarily in the Bible. Otherwise, demographic data, surveys, and marketing techniques may lead the church away from its true identity and divinely given mission.

According to Paul S. Minear in his classic study *Images of the Church in the New Testament,* more than eighty images of the church appear in the New Testament, by a conservative estimation. Four images, however, dominate the New Testament's description of the church: people of God, the new creation, the fellowship in faith, and the body of Christ.

The People of God

The images that cluster around the conception of the church as *the people of God* place the church in the setting of the long story of God's dealing with the chosen people. "You are a chosen race, a royal priesthood, a holy nation, God's own people, in order that you may proclaim the mighty acts of him who called you out of darkness into his marvelous light" (1 Peter 2:9; *see* Romans 9:25-26). The church is in the same long tradition as the Law and the Prophets and shares the same heritage and mission as the "Israel of God" (Galatians 6:15-16).

The church is a "holy nation," rooted in a covenantal relationship with God and set apart for special purposes. It is "Abraham's offspring" (Galatians 3:29; Romans 4:16), and as such the church shares in Abraham's posterity. The original covenant with and promise to Abraham was that he was to be a means by which God blessed all the families of the earth (Genesis 12:2-3). God had sworn to bring many nations into this one promise. In the new age brought by Christ, Gentiles are included as children of Abraham and heirs of the covenantal promise (Galatians 3:28-29).

The existence of the people of God, the church, is due to God's own initiative, not the merits or power or prestige of the people. It is by God's grace that the church, the people of God, are created, called, sustained, judged, and saved (Romans 9:19-33; 11:5).

Other terms revolve around the central image of *the people of God. Flock* is widely used (Matthew 26:31; Luke 12:32; John 10:16; Acts 20:28-29; 1 Corinthians 9:7; 1 Peter 5:2-3). The church is viewed as God's flock with Jesus as the shepherd (Hebrews 13:20). "Do not be afraid, little flock, for it is your Father's good pleasure to give you the kingdom" (Luke 12:32).

The flock owes its existence to the shepherd who calls each sheep by name, seeks them when they go astray, guides them into the fold. Christ is the Good Shepherd, who seeks to bring other sheep into the same fold (John 10:16), who cares for sheep who have no shepherd (Mark 6:34), and who gathers lost sheep (Matthew 10:6; 15:24). There is a strong interdependence between the flock and the Shepherd, and the relationship is characterized by trust and compassion.

Other images or metaphors for *the people of God* come from religious traditions. The *temple,* as a dwelling place of God's Spirit, refers not only to the body of individual believers (as in 1 Corinthians 6:19) but also to *congregations* of believers (as in 1 Corinthians 3:16-17). In Ephesians 2:19-22 the image of a temple is extended to describe the *whole church.* First Peter 2:5 speaks of Christians as "living stones" built into a "spiritual house." Jesus Christ, of course, is the cornerstone (Ephesians 2:20).

The New Creation

A second dominant image of the church in the New Testament is *the new creation.* As the images of the people of God set the church in the context of the covenant history of Israel, the images of the new creation set the church in a universal or cosmic context. The same God who acts within a particular covenant history also acts within the whole human family and all of creation. God's purpose in choosing a particular people is to accomplish universal and cosmic purposes.

The church is composed of those who live as a "new creation": "If anyone is in Christ, there is a new creation; everything old has passed away; see, everything has become new!" (2 Corinthians 5:17). Christ represents a new creation, the first fruits of a new humanity (1 Corinthians 15:20-23). The Spirit is at work within the Christian community as a guarantee of the coming redemption of the whole creation (Romans 8:23). As Minear writes, "The Christian community as a whole is begotten in order to serve as the first fruits of all God's creatures."[1]

The image of the church as the first fruits of a new creation reflects the church's mission to the world. The church lives between what God has done and what God will do in all creation. It identifies Jesus Christ as the agent through whom God is at work. The church is linked to God the Creator, to Christ "the firstborn of all creation" (Colossians 1:15), and to the whole creation.

Linked to the image of the new creation is the picture of *the new humanity.* "You have stripped off the old self with its practices and have clothed yourselves with the new self, which is being renewed in knowledge according to the image of its creator. In that renewal there is no longer Greek and Jew, circumcised and uncircumcised, barbarian, Scythian, slave and free; but Christ is all and in all!" (Colossians 3:9-11).

The new humanity is not a private, individualistic matter so much as a communal or corporate reality. And that communal reality grows in conformity to the image of God in Christ. Christ was "created according to the likeness of God" (Ephesians 4:24) and has "broken down the dividing wall, that is, the hostility, . . . that he might create in himself one new humanity in place of the two" (Ephesians 2:14-15). Jesus Christ is the image of this new creation and new humanity. All who belong to Christ will bear his image as they are being renewed and transformed, "from one degree of glory to another" (2 Corinthians 3:18).

Another biblical way of talking about the new creation is in terms of the kingdom of God. "Jesus came to Galilee, proclaiming the good news of God, saying, 'The time is fulfilled, and the kingdom of God has come near' " (Mark 1:14-15). The kingdom of God comes as God's new heaven and new earth, and it is God's gift rather than a human achievement (Luke 12:32). The reign of God has already been set in motion in the person and ministry of Jesus Christ.

In the New Testament the kingdom of God was understood as the opposite of the kingdom of Satan, evil. Now persons must make a radical choice between the two kingdoms, which continue to struggle for dominance.

Those who inherit the Kingdom and have a special place within it include the despised, the poor, the meek, the hungry, the persecuted; but the heirs become rich and blessed, beloved and joyful, as they share in the reign of God (Matthew

5:3-10; 22:1-10; Luke 6:20-23; 14:16-24; 1 Corinthians 1:26-30; James 2:5). Judgment in the Kingdom involves responsiveness to the hungry, the thirsty, the stranger, the naked, the sick, and the imprisoned; for service "to one of the least of these" is service to Christ (Matthew 25:31-46). The church exists as a visible sign, foretaste, and herald of the coming of God's reign of justice, generosity, love, and joy; therefore, its faithfulness is judged by how closely it resembles God's coming reign brought near in the life, teachings, death, and resurrection of Jesus Christ.

The Fellowship in Faith

A third dominant image of the church is *the fellowship in faith.* The church is the fellowship of the *saints.* Paul addressed a letter to the church in Corinth "to those who are sanctified in Christ Jesus" and "called to be saints" (1 Corinthians 1:2). No fewer than one hundred passages in eighteen different writings speak of church members as *saints.*

As the company of saints, the church depends on the ongoing activity of God. It is God's holiness that the church shares (Hebrews 12:10). Because the One who called the church into being is holy, the church must be holy (1 Peter 1:15-16). The church's holiness, or sanctification, is related to Christ's sacrificial death. "We have been sanctified through the offering of the body of Jesus Christ once and for all" (Hebrews 10:10, 14, 29; 13:12; Ephesians 5:26).

When the church is spoken of as the saints, the power of the Holy Spirit is assumed to be at work within it. The community has been born of the Spirit and baptized into one Spirit. The Spirit is poured out on the community, and the Spirit dwells within it.

The community is described in such terms as *believers, the faithful,* and *those who have trusted or believed in the name* (John 1:12; 3:15; 5:24; 17:20-21; Acts 2:44; 4:4, 32; 5:14; Romans 3:22; 1 Corinthians 14:22; Ephesians 1:19; Colossians 1:2; Hebrews 4:3; 1 Peter 2:7; Revelation 17:14).

The act of believing creates a new person who lives in a new community in a new age. Therefore, the believers are bound together with new bonds. They are bound together by a new boldness (Acts 4:10-20), a unanimity of praise and prayer (4:23-31), a transformation in the idea of property and concern for others' needs (2:44-45), a new mutuality and hospitality (Romans 14:3; 15:7). They must treat every person as one for whom Christ died, and accordingly they must avoid any action that would injure another (14:13-15). They must give priority to the common good and to God's work in building up the household of faith rather than to self-esteem and self-interest. They must help to bear the burden of those who are weak in the faith (15:1-3). They must live in such harmony with one another that their life together will glorify God (15:6).

As *the fellowship in faith,* the church is made up of *followers* and *disciples.* The church is composed not merely of people who like one another but of those who follow after and learn about Jesus Christ. Among the requirements of discipleship laid down by Jesus are these: to take up the cross, to lose one's life for Christ's sake, to reduce to secondary status obligations to kinfolk, to refuse to count the cost in advance (Matthew 10:37-38; Mark 8:34; Luke 9:57-62; 14:26-33).

The rules of this fellowship are peculiar. Since the disciples have one master, they are on one level of genuine equality: brothers or sisters to one another (Matthew 23:8-10). Even more disturbing, among the fellowship of disciples, the last shall be first and the first last, reversing the usual standards of inferiority and superiority (Matthew 23:11-12; Mark 10:35-45).

The Body of Christ

The fourth prevalent image of the church in the New Testament is *the body of Christ.* This image is found explicitly only in Paul's Letters. The meaning of the image varies; and it is difficult, if not impossible, to reduce it to one definition.

Among the many uses that Paul makes of the body imagery is that of affirming the diversity of the ministries of the Christian community (1 Corinthians 12–14). In every spiritual gift there must be oneness in source and goal: "There are varieties of gifts, but the same Spirit" (12:4). Every gift has been given for the sake of the common good, not for the edification of the individual. Paul uses the body image in 1 Corinthians 12:14 as a way of conveying the truth that all the gifts "are activated by one and the same Spirit, who allots to each one individually just as the Spirit chooses" (12:11).

All have been baptized into one body; and this baptism has destroyed the old solidarities of race, class, and ranking. It is an incorporation into a body of interdependent members and mutual sharing of the Spirit's variety of gifts. "Just as the body is one and has many members, and all the members of the body, though many, are one body, so it is with Christ" (12:12).

"Now you are the body of Christ and individually members of it" (1 Corinthians 12:27). This mutual relation to Christ creates the sense of interdependence among the members. There is absolute solidarity. "If one member suffers, all suffer together with it; if one member is honored, all rejoice together with it" (12:26). Such unity results from sharing in Christ's own life and work.

The imagery of the body makes clear that Christ is the head of the church. "In him the whole fullness of deity dwells bodily, and you have come to fullness in him, who is the head of every ruler and authority" (Colossians 2:9-10). It is Christ who exercises authority over the church and over all creation. Christ is the creative source of the church's life, the One in whom and through whom and for whom the church is created (1:12-13).

The image of the body of Christ as described in Colossians portrays the church as a new society. The boundaries that separated Greeks from Jews, barbarians from Scythians, slaves from free people had been transcended. "A new society had appeared that transformed the criteria of social judgment, the bases of social cohesion, and the structures of social institutions. . . . The truth embodied in Christ's headship and the church's bodyhood was an explosive force, designed to shatter all other conceptions of social organization and historical process."[2]

The Letter to the Colossians makes an important point about *growth* of the body of Christ. Colossians does not relate the picture of the growing body to numerical increase of membership. Growth is in terms of the body's dominion over darkness and death (Colossians 3:5). The body grows when people hold fast to the head (Christ) and when from this head the whole

body is "nourished and held together" (2:19). It grows when it allows the word of Christ to dwell in it richly and as it obeys the command of Christ to "teach and admonish one another" and "with gratitude in your hearts sing psalms, hymns, and spiritual songs to God" (3:16). Through the practice of mutuality—compassion, patience, forgiveness, love—the body grows.

The work of building up the body was designed to present every person as a whole person, fully developed and "mature in Christ" (1:28). It is the head of the body (Christ) who makes such work possible through the indwelling presence of the Holy Spirit. Growth then is nothing less than the maturity of the body as it is empowered and directed by its head. Only a church shaped by the image of Christ is the mature body of Christ.

WHAT THE *DISCIPLINE* SAYS
(*Discipline,* Part III, ¶¶ 120–132; student book, pages 55–59)

The Mission and Ministry of the Church

Grounded in Scripture, The United Methodist Church understands itself as a covenant community summoned by God's self-revelation in the life, death, and resurrection of Jesus Christ to ministry in the world. As a covenant community shaped and empowered by the Holy Spirit, we are called together for worship and fellowship and for upbuilding the Christian community as a visible sign, foretaste, and herald of God's reign brought near and assured in the life, teachings, death, resurrection, and final victory of Jesus Christ.

The *Discipline* affirms: "The heart of Christian ministry is Christ's ministry of outreaching love. Christian ministry is the expression of the mind and mission of Christ by a community of Christians that demonstrates a common life of gratitude and devotion, witness and service, celebration and discipleship. All Christians are called through their baptism to this ministry of servanthood in the world to the glory of God . . ." (¶ 125; student book, page 57). Through the church, we are invited as recipients of and participants in God's mission of reconciling and transforming the world. The ultimate concern is "that all persons will be brought into a saving relationship with God through Jesus Christ and be renewed after the image of their creator (Colossians 3:10)" (¶ 126; student book, page 57.)

The church's ministry, though diverse in its expression and contexts, is one ministry and is both a gift and a task. The ministry is first and foremost God's ministry, which we have been graciously invited to receive and share. Baptism is our initiation into God's ministry through the church, and it represents the unity of all ministry. Ordination is, therefore, not to be seen as supplanting baptism or bestowing a superior status of ministry. "The ministry of all Christians is complementary. No ministry is subservient to another. All United Methodists are summoned and sent by Christ to live and work together in mutual interdependence and to be guided by the Spirit into the truth that frees and the love that reconciles" (¶ 129; student book, page 58). Ministry is a life of servanthood, which is both privilege and obligation, nurtured by ongoing relationship with God and accountable Christian discipleship (¶¶ 133–35; student book, pages 59–60).

The United Methodist Church is a *connectional* church. Connectionalism is an expression of our theology and our strategy for mission; it is not primarily a description of our organizational structure. Connectional structures are visible expressions of mutual interdependency within the body of Christ. No local congregation, church agency, or denomination can contain fully the body of Christ or fulfill Christ's comprehensive mission. The *Discipline* states, "Connectionalism in the United Methodist tradition is multi-leveled, global in scope, and local in thrust. Our connectionalism is . . . a vital web of interactive relationships" (¶ 130; student book, page 58).

The *Discipline* states the mission of the church succinctly: "to make disciples of Jesus Christ by proclaiming the good news of God's grace and thus seeking the fulfillment of God's reign and realm in the world" (¶ 121; student book, pages 55–56). Although making disciples of Jesus Christ is the global mission of the church and the priority of all its institutional expression, local churches are the primary "arena through which disciple-making occurs" and "a strategic base from which Christians move out to the structures of society" (¶¶ 120 and 202; student book, pages 55, 63).

The Identity and Mission of the Church and Our Theological Task

The church is a community of people who out of gratitude for and commitment to God's grace live toward the vision God has for the world. The church seeks to be a community of grace, an outpost of God's new creation. As such, it seeks to understand the nature and purpose of God and to clarify its perception of God's vision for humankind and all creation. Such the church exists as a sign and herald of God's presence and purposes, it must be grounded in and shaped by understanding of and commitment to the God who calls the church into being.

Doctrinal understanding and theological reflection, therefore, are central activities of the church, not peripheral, intellectual sideshows. If we fail to understand our doctrinal and theological heritage and framework, we lose our unique identity as the church. Without an awareness of the doctrines and faith of our heritage, the church becomes a religious institution with amnesia and without vision. Such an institution becomes at best a fellowship of nice people trying to be nicer or at worst a reactionary or revolutionary obstacle to God's purposes.

Recovery of images of the church grounded in Scripture and historic Christian doctrine as professed in the Wesleyan tradition can help the church avoid becoming merely one more social institution competing for the time, energies, and financial resources of its members. An identity and mission grounded in relationship with God in Christ and committed to the purposes of God will enable the church to be a means by which God transforms the world into the divine image.

The task of refining the church's identity, ministry, and mission as God's community is the responsibility of the whole church, not just of theologians or pastors or denominational executives. Our theological statement affirms, "United Methodists as a diverse people continue to strive for consensus in understanding the gospel. In our diversity, we are held together by a shared inheritance and a common desire to participate in the creative and redemptive activity of God" (*Discipline*, ¶ 104; student book, page 52).

This study is an invitation—an invitation to explore our shared faith inheritance, to sharpen our understanding and experience of the gospel, and to participate in the ongoing gift of knowing the reality of God and participating in God's grace-filled mission to the world.

THE SESSION PLAN

1. Since this is the introductory session, you may need to spend time getting acquainted. To introduce the subject matter while building fellowship in the group, prepare in advance special name tags. On half of the tags, print or type, in addition to a place for the name, a term from the glossary on pages 65–72 of the student book. On the other half of the name tags, print or type a corresponding definition of the term from the glossary. Pass out the tags. Ask participants to write in their own name and then find the person who matches their term or definition. For example, the match for "Laity" would be "The people of God (*laos* means 'people'). The term is traditionally applied to those members of the church who are not ordained (the clergy)."

After a few minutes, have class members assemble. Introduce the session with a statement similar to the following: "Hold on to your name tag. If you are already familiar with the concept on it, maybe your understanding will deepen. If you have a term that remains confusing, maybe together we can discover its meaning. We have come together to discover more clearly who we are as United Methodist Christians and what it means to be the church. We will be considering together the doctrinal/theological statement of The United Methodist Church. It is an invitation to explore basic Christian beliefs and the identity and mission of the church. The goal is not simply to study beliefs but to explore our own faith and relationship with God."

2. Distribute copies of the student book.

3. Begin with a consideration of how the church differs from other institutions or organizations of which we are a part. Have group members compare three institutions—a fast-food restaurant (for profit), a civic club (not for profit), and the church. Write the following characteristics on separate index cards:

Purpose: to earn profit.
Purpose: fellowship and voluntary service.
Purpose: faithfulness to God's purposes.
Organization: personnel selected by management and corporate headquarters.
Organization: officers and committees elected by membership.
Organization: determined by denomination and local congregation.
Facilities: kitchen, dining room.
Facilities: room at local restaurant.
Facilities: varied, may meet in special facilities, or in homes.
Measures of Success: number of customers, profits.
Measures of Success: membership size, attendance, dues collected, volunteers for projects
Measures of Success: faithfulness to God, growth in Christlikeness.
Motivation: to satisfy appetites, to earn profits.
Motivation: fellowship based on similar interests.
Motivation: gratitude for God's grace and commitment to God's purposes.
Methods for Determining Expansion: market surveys of people's tastes and habits.
Methods for Determining Expansion: ideas of members.
Methods for Determining Expansion: discernment of will of God in context of local and global needs.
How to Grow: advertising, offer what customers want, stress convenience.
How to Grow: members invite new members.
How to Grow: growth difficult to measure by statistics but related to love for God and neighbor.

You may think of other categories or characteristics. Put them on separate index cards also. Distribute the cards to class members. Write the three headings—*Fast-Food Restaurant, Civic Club,*

Church—on a sheet of posterboard. Ask members to tape under the appropriate heading the characteristics on his or her card.

Talk about areas of similarity and difference. Explain that the characteristics listed under *Church* are the ideal. In reality, the church may operate more like a fast-food restaurant or a civic club. Where does your local church fit? Spend some time talking as a group about the consequences of thinking of the church primarily as a social organization.

Possible points to raise: Church members may see themselves as "belonging to" the church in the same way that they belong to a civic club or the institution for which they work. The notion that the church is something they *are* eludes them. Church participation involves activities, programs, events sponsored by the organization called the church. Church loyalty is measured by the level of participation in those activities, programs, and events. Service to the church is rendered by supporting the institutional needs of the organization—ushering, committee membership, teaching, giving money, and the like.

When the church is defined primarily by its institutional characteristics, success is measured in terms of statistical growth; and ministry is seen as service to the institution. Membership gain, attendance increases, and financial outlay become the outward and visible signs of faithfulness. The absence of such signs of progress results in proposals to reverse the statistics. Most of the proposals consist of recommendations for changes in structure, methods, leadership style, management techniques, personnel deployment. They sound like efforts to rescue a declining business rather than a summons to faithfulness to a God-given identity and vision.

When the church is defined primarily by its institutional qualities, evangelism is equated with church growth, and commitment is reduced to maintaining the institution. Getting *persons into the church* receives more emphasis than getting *the church into the world*. Marketing techniques replace the proclamation of the gospel in word and deed as primary tools of evangelism. Effective recruitment methods take on more importance than the message of the faith. Ministry consists of responding to persons' wants and preferences rather than being transforming agents in society.

An institutionally defined church views *mission* as preserving the power and position of the institution. The United Methodist Church began as a mission or movement, and its organization and structure were adopted as means of accomplishing its mission of reforming the nation and spreading scriptural holiness throughout the land. Now, however, the mission tends to be defined in terms of maintaining and strengthening the structure, the institution.

4. As another way of prompting discussing of what the church *is* and what the church *does*, read aloud the following story, entitled "Lying Offshore."

A ship rocked slowly upon the greasy seas. Its sails were tattered, its masts spliced, and its hull leaky with worm-eaten planks, but still it stayed afloat. It had been sailing for many years—for generations actually. Many years ago it had been loaded with food and medicine, and dispatched to find and to help the people of a lost colony. As it traveled far and wide, all its original crew except one had died, their places being taken by their children.

In the prow an old man, the last of the original crew, sat upon a coil of rope, his watery eyes struggling to pierce the fog.

Below decks men, women, and children sat down to eat. Although their fare was meager, it was adequate, and all their faces shone with health.

The meal was almost over when both doors of the messroom were thrown open with a loud noise and a rush of wind. In the opening stood the old man, strange and wild, stronger than they had ever seen him, shouting, "We're *here!* We've arrived at land!"

"Land?" they asked, not moving from the table, "what land?"

"Why the land we were sent to when this voyage began. And the lost colony is there waiting. I can hear them shouting from the shore!" shouted the old man, stamping his feet with impatience. "Quick! Let's make for shore and unload the food and the medicine!"

The old man turned to run back up the gangway, but stopped halfway up when he realized there had been no movement in the messroom. Slowly he returned to stare at them with wide, incredulous eyes, his mouth agape. "Didn't you hear me? Are you all deaf? I said we're here! The people we were sent out to help are only a few hundred yards away. But we must hurry, for they are all hungry and sick."

"I'm sure we'd all like to help those people," said one of the men, "but—as you can see—there's hardly enough food and medicine here to take care of us and our children."

"Besides," said one of the women, "we don't know what kind of people they are. Who knows *what* might happen if we landed and went among them?"

The old man staggered back as if he had been struck across the face. "But . . . but . . . it was for *them* that this voyage began in the first place so many years ago, for *them* that the ship was built, for *them* that the food and medicine were stowed aboard!"

"Yes, old man. I've heard *many* tales of our launching from my father and from the other old men who are now dead," replied one of the younger men, "but there were so many different accounts that how can we be sure which one is right? Why risk our stores and provisions, perhaps even our lives, on something we may not even be supposed to do?"

"He's right! He's right!" shouted many of the others, now quite excitedly involved in the conversation.

"But look," said the old man, trying very hard to contain himself, "it's all very simple! As far as there not being enough food for us *and* them, much of what we have left is meant for *seed*. If we go ashore and *plant* it, then there will be more than enough for all. And on the matter of *why* the ship was launched in the first place—you have merely to look in the logbook. It's all there."

The old man, hoping he had settled the question, looked anxiously from face to face around the tables. There was a long, thoughtful silence.

Finally, a man who had gravitated to a position of leadership among them stood up, picking his teeth and frowning thoughtfully.

"Perhaps the old man is right," he said, loosening a juicy morsel from between two teeth. "At any rate, his suggestion merits investigation. What I propose is this: let us select from among ourselves a representative committee which will see if they can find the old logbook, and then go into a thorough study of it, to see if they can determine whether we should land or not."

"A sensible idea!" they all cried, except the old man. "Let's do it!"

The old man, now frantic with hearing the cries from shore, shouted, "What *is* this? What are you *doing*? Oh!" he said, backing away from them with horror in his eyes, "I can see that you do not really expect to do anything at all!" His back against a bulkhead, he clutched at his chest and slid weakly to the floor.

"Let me warn you then," he gasped. "The food will not last. It was meant to stay preserved only for the time it would take to get here. Now the food will begin to molder, and the medicines will separate and lose their strength. If you do not take the provisions ashore and share them, they will soon no longer feed or cure even you!" With this, he died.

As the days and weeks passed, the ship continued to lie offshore. The committee continued to search the logbook, which they had soon found, hoping to come up with a report "in the near future." A few of the younger men and women, maddened with the waiting and lured irresistibly by the cries of hunger and pain from the shore, slipped away one night in the jolly boat with a few provisions, and were listed sorrowfully next day as "lost at sea."

True to the old man's dying prophecy, the food on board began to grow all manner of weird and exotic fungi, and the extensive stores of medicine seemed less and less able to cure the ills of the people. Also, the cries from the shore began to grow so much louder that even the deafest on board had to stuff his ears with cotton in order to sleep.

But no one seemed to be able to decide what to do.[3]

Ask the class this question: According to the story, what is the basic problem of the modern church? (Possible answers: loss of identity, preoccupation with its own self, apathy about mission, substituting study for action, fear of people who are different, ministry of self-serving or institutional preservation.)

5. The primary source for understanding the church's identity is the Bible. Spend some time reviewing the four major biblical images of the church: the people of God, the new creation, the fellowship in faith, and the body of Christ. Divide the class into four teams with Bibles and the following lists. Ask team members to look up the key passages under their assigned heading:

People of God:
Genesis 12:2-3; Matthew 10:6; 15:24; 26:31; Mark 6:3-4; Luke 2:8; 12:32; John 10:16; Acts 20:28-29; Romans 4:16; 9:19-33; 11:5; 1 Corinthians 3:16-17; 6:19; 9:7; Galatians 3:28-29; 6:15-16; Ephesians 2:20; Hebrews 13:20; 1 Peter 2:5, 9; 5:2-3

New Creation:
Matthew 5:3-10; 22:1-10; 25:31-46; Mark 1:14-15; Luke 6:20-23; 12:32; 14:16-24; Romans 8:23; 1 Corinthians 1:26-30; 15:20-23; 2 Corinthians 3:18; 5:17; Ephesians 2:14-15; 4:24; Colossians 1:15-16; 3:10; James 2:5

Fellowship in Faith:
Matthew 10:37-38; 23:8-12; Mark 8:34; 10:35-45; Luke 9:57-62; 14:26-33; John 1:12; 3:15; 5:24; 17:20-21; Acts 2:44-45; 4:4, 10-20, 23-32; 5:14; Romans 3:22; 14:3, 13-15; 15:1-3, 7; 18:6; 1 Corinthians 1:2; 14:22; Ephesians 1:19; 5:26; Colossians 1:2; Hebrews 4:3; 10:10, 14, 29; 12:10; 13:12; 1 Peter 1:15-16; 2:7; Revelation 17:14

Body of Christ:
1 Corinthians 12–14; Colossians 1:12-13, 28-29; 2:9-10, 19; 3:5, 15-16

Allow several minutes for this Bible study. Then invite members to review the material in the earlier section "What the *Discipline* Says" in light of the Bible study.

6. For this step you will need to have on hand supplies such as paper, colored felt-tip pens, modeling clay, magazines with pictures, scissors, glue, pipe cleaners, string, and the like. Ask each team to create a visual image (drawing, model, picture) that depicts the assigned image. For example, the *people of God* might be portrayed either as a flock of sheep with Christ as the shepherd, as a temple, or as Abraham and his descendants. *New creation* might be portrayed as a caterpillar and butterfly, as a fruit-bearing tree, or as a broken-down wall. The *fellowship in faith* lends itself to the imagery of a household, a group of disciples who sit at Jesus' feet, or one Christian serving another. The *body of Christ* could be depicted as a human body with Christ as the head. Names of church members, denominations, or church agencies could be written on the figure.

Ask teams to display the results of their work and to give a brief explanation of what the symbolism means. Be familiar with the material in this leader's guide under "Grounding in Scripture" and "What the *Discipline* Says" and be prepared to add to the implications under each image.

7. Have members read the *Discipline,* Part III, ¶¶ 120–29, from the student book, pages 55–58. Ask, Where do you see the biblical images of the church present in this description of the church? In what ways does the description in the *Discipline* clarify the biblical images?

8. To close, have members turn to Article V in the Confession of Faith of The Evangelical United Brethren Church, page 35 in the student book. Read the article in unison as an affirmation of faith.

---

[1] *Images of the Church in the New Testament,* by Paul S. Minear (The Westminster Press, 1960), page 112.

[2] *Images of the Church in the New Testament,* page 211.

[3] "Lying Offshore" from *The Innovator and Other Modern Parables,* by G. William Jones (Abingdon Press, 1969), pages 35–38. Reprinted by permission of the author.

OUR ROOTS RUN DEEP

Purpose of This Session:

To help adults recognize that United Methodism is in the mainstream of historic Christian witness and theology.

Goals of This Session:

1. To introduce adults to some basic foundational, ecumenical documents, especially the creeds, as necessary resources for understanding the Christian faith.
2. To help adults appreciate that current efforts to define beliefs and stimulate theological exploration are built upon past attempts to do the same.
3. To encourage adults to examine their own personal faith in light of the great creeds and other historic affirmations.

GROUNDING IN SCRIPTURE

The foundation document of the church is the Bible itself. It contains statements of faith, creedal formulations, and is a source and a parameter for the historic creeds of the church.

Creeds are belief statements or summaries of basic beliefs. They attempt to capture in memorable form important affirmations of a religious community. As such, they are subject to clarification and revision. In addition to statements of belief, certain liturgical materials, such as hymns and prayers, take on the function of a creed. They capture the essence of belief about God or an aspect of God's nature or activity.

The Bible contains summaries of such creedal affirmations. For example, the "song of Moses" (Exodus 15:1-18) and the "song of Miriam" (15:21) are early affirmations of God's mighty act of deliverance from Egypt. Many scholars contend that Miriam's song is the older or original affirmation of the Exodus event. The song of Moses probably represents an embellishment of the song by subsequent writers as they included other signs of God's triumph over Israel's foes.

The Shema is a concise statement of faith of the people of Israel: "Hear, O Israel: The LORD is our God, the LORD alone. You shall love the LORD your God with all your heart, and with all your soul, and with all your might" (Detueronomy 6:4-5). There follows the admonition that the precepts are to be learned and passed on to the next generation (6:6-9).

The Ten Commandments may be viewed as creedal formulations (Exodus 20:2-17; Deuteronomy 5:6-21). The numerous additional laws in Leviticus and Deuteronomy may be seen as expansions and interpretations of the foundational ten laws.

Hymns and prayers for varied personal and communal occasions are found in the Book of Psalms. They were part of the collective life of the congregation and were preserved for their liturgical and creedal value by Jews and Christians. They are *means* of expressing the community's feelings before God, and they also are *expressions* of the community's faith in God.

The New Testament builds upon the historic affirmations of the Old Testament. It too contains brief summary affirmations of the church's faith. For example, Peter's confession at Caesarea Philippi summarizes the early church's belief about Jesus: "You are the Messiah, the Son of the living God" (Matthew 16:16; see also Mark 8:29; Luke 9:20). One might argue that Mark contains the oldest affirmation, "You are the Messiah," and that

Matthew and Luke expand upon it in light of the issues they confronted. Philippians 2:3-11, according to some scholars, is a hymn about Christ that the early church may have used to express belief in the incarnation of God in Christ.

Paul's letters reflect the Bible's dual practice of preserving historic parameters of beliefs while reevaluating those beliefs in light of contemporary issues and situations. Paul's analogy of the olive tree is a good example (Romans 11:17-24). God's promises are known and affirmed in and through the traditions of Israel. Christ made possible the "grafting" of an additional branch into this tree of tradition. The church, as Paul affirmed, was rooted in the promises of God to Abraham and his descendants, but Christ made new affirmations necessary.

The Bible contains many statements that continue to function as creeds or affirmations of faith. For example, the following passages are treated as such in *The United Methodist Hymnal* approved by the 1988 General Conference: Romans 8:35, 37-39; 1 Corinthians 15:1-6; Colossians 1:15-20; 1 Timothy 1:15; 2:5-6; 3:16.

In addition to being a primary source of creeds, Scripture supports the basic affirmations of the historic ecumenical creeds. The Apostles' Creed affirms God as Creator (Genesis 1–2; Isaiah 42:5; 45:18). It declares that Jesus is God's Son (Matthew 3:17; Mark 1:1, 11; 3:11; 5:7; 15:39; Luke 1:35; 4:41; 8:28; John 1:34, 49; 3:16-18; 10:36; 11:27; 20:31). He was "conceived by the Holy Spirit, born of the Virgin Mary" (Matthew 1:18; Luke 1:26-38), "suffered under Pontius Pilate, was crucified, dead and buried" (Matthew 27; Mark 15; Luke 23; John 19). "The third day he rose from the dead; he ascended into heaven" (Matthew 28; Mark 16; Luke 24; John 20–21; 1 Corinthians 15). "From thence he shall come to judge the quick and the dead" (1 Thessalonians 4:14-17; 5:23). Belief in "the Holy Spirit, the holy catholic church, the communion of saints, the forgiveness of sins, the resurrection of the body, and the life everlasting" clearly are rooted in the New Testament.

The Nicene Creed makes affirmations similar to those of the Apostles' Creed, although in more abstract philosophical language. Its basic concepts are deeply rooted in the New Testament. Some of its terminology, however, can be traced to Greek philosophy, such as "begotten, not made, of one Being with the Father; through him all things were made."

The basic tenets of the Protestant Reformation are likewise found upon Scripture (see references on pages 19–20). As subsequent sessions show, salvation by grace is a pivotal New Testament concept, especially in the Letters of Paul (Romans 5–6; Ephesians 2:4-10). The authority of Scripture in matters of faith is supported by the fact that we depend on the Bible for the witness to God's self-revelation in the history of Israel and in Jesus Christ. The priesthood of all believers is affirmed by the biblical understanding of the very nature of the church as the people of God, the body of Christ, the new creation, and the fellowship in faith.

WHAT THE *DISCIPLINE* SAYS
(*Discipline*, ¶ 101; student book, pages 7–17)

The theological statement rightfully claims "Our forebears in the faith reaffirmed the ancient Christian message as found in the apostolic [*New Testament and early church*] witness, even as they applied it anew in their own circumstances" (*Discipline*, ¶ 101; student book, page 7). United Methodists share a common heritage with all Christians. Therefore, the historic creeds and doctrines play a significant role in defining who we are.

The historic ecumenical creeds and the crucial foundation documents are sources of God's truth. They also help to establish the parameters of basic Christian doctrine. We begin to clarify our identity as United Methodists not with Wesley but with the longer tradition that Wesley himself accepted and built upon.

Role and Purpose of Creeds

Creeds traditionally have served several important functions in the church. They originally were vehicles by which the baptized were taught the faith and affirmed their faith. The creeds were aimed partly at excluding false doctrine by defining briefly and precisely what are considered to be legitimate beliefs. They became, then, criteria or yardsticks by which new theological presuppositions were evaluated.

Creeds also serve as teaching tools and as means of passing the faith on to succeeding generations. They are gifts of the past to the present. As gifts, they deserve to be treated with respect while also being used and shared. They require reevaluation and reapplication in each generation. They are like usable heirlooms received from valued forebears. They connect us to the past, provide models for new creations, and inspire additional creativity.

Creeds also serve the purposes of evangelism and witness. A creed is, in the words of one United Methodist theologian, "an affirmation or avowal of loyalty."[1] Creeds, then, are means of commitment and communal pledges of loyalty to the God made known in Jesus Christ and proclaimed by the community of faith. Creeds are means of declaring to the world our commitment to live in accordance with the God of Jesus Christ.

Creeds provide a place to stand when the winds of theology are blowing in all directions. They are docks from which new expeditions may be launched and to which pilgrims return for instruction and direction.

A friend of mine was a prisoner of war for almost four years in the 1940's. He tells of the desperate struggle to maintain his sanity and his hope. When asked to identify the resources that enabled him to survive, he said, "My faith was one resource. I had particular beliefs that I had learned from my parents and my church. I kept repeating those in my mind. Things like the Lord's Prayer, John 3:16, the Apostles' Creed, kept me in touch with who I was." Those basic affirmations provided a firm foundation when all about him was crumbling.

Historic creeds and confessions of faith serve a similar role for the Christian community, which often finds itself a prisoner within an alien and pagan culture.

United Methodists' Doctrinal Roots

Methodism began as a movement within the Anglican tradition, and it remained within the doctrinal framework of that tradition. It was significantly influenced by other traditions, however, especially German pietism and certain strands of the Reformed tradition. The United Methodist Church, formed in 1968, uniquely welded a rich diversity of doctrinal backgrounds, as Philip William Otterbein, Martin Boehm, Jacob Albright, and their heirs joined John and Charles Wesley, Thomas Coke, and Francis Asbury in that endless splendor of noble heroes of the new church.

John Wesley was probably as well versed in the writings of the early church leaders (apostolic fathers) as any person alive in eighteenth-century England. He considered himself within the mainstream of historical theology. He sought to establish no new denomination but rather to reemphasize the essential tenets of the faith as preached by the apostolic witnesses. Wesley stressed the importance of reading the works of the saints of the church down through the centuries.

Wesley checked his own interpretations against the great interpreters of the past. He wrote to William Dodd, "In your last paragraph you say, 'You set aside all authority, ancient and modern.' Sir, who told you so? I never did; it never entered my thoughts. Who it was gave you that rule I know not; but my father gave it me thirty years ago (I mean concerning reverence to the ancient church and our own), and I have endeavored to walk by it to this day. But I try every doctrine by the Bible."[2]

United Methodists exhibit in their theology and doctrine an appreciation of the broader scope of church history. They live in the mainstreams of doctrine and belief flowing from the long history of Christendom.

Ecumenical Creeds and Foundation Documents

The theological statement contends that "the adoption of ecumenical creeds such as the formulations of Nicaea and Chalcedon were of central importance. . . . Such creeds helped preserve the integrity of the church's witness, set boundaries for acceptable Christian doctrine, and proclaimed the basic elements of the enduring Christian message" (*Discipline*, ¶101; student book, page 8).

The exact origins of the Apostles' and Nicene Creeds have been debated. In general it is agreed that the so-called Apostles' Creed, which took its traditional name from the legend that the twelve apostles composed it by each writing in turn one of its twelve clauses, goes back to the type of baptismal confession used by the Latin-speaking churches of western Europe. Its modern form is similar to the "Old Roman Creed" of around A.D. 340.

The Nicene Creed dates back to the early baptismal confessions of faith of the Eastern Church. It was originally presented and formulated at the Second Ecumenical Council at Constantinople, A.D. 381, and was ratified as authoritative for the eastern and western parts of the church at the Fourth Ecumenical Council at Chalcedon, A.D. 451. It is called "Nicene" because it contains the essential doctrinal formula declared by the First Ecumenical Council at Nicaea in A.D. 325. It is partly an attempt to repudiate the heretical notion that Christ was semidivine.

Both the Apostles' Creed and the Nicene Creed place emphasis upon the triune God. Very early in the church, a confession of the triune name—Father, Son, and Holy Spirit (Holy Ghost)—became the essential and accepted baptismal confession. Some apostolic leaders contended that the formula originated in the directive of the risen Christ (Matthew 28:19). From these baptismal creeds and triune formula came the later formalized Apostles' Creed and Nicene Creed.

The Heidelberg Catechism, another historic creedal formulation, generally has been traced to around 1563 when the theological faculty at Heidelberg was asked to formulate a confession. Over a period of about fifty years, it was widely accepted among the Reformed Churches. It continually goes back to the Bible as its authority, and it closely connects the moral life of the Christian with faith. Its emphasis is on the authority of Scripture and holy living, which are dominant strains in the Methodist tradition.

In addition to the Apostles' Creed, the Nicene Creed, and the Heidelberg Catechism, two additional documents are foundational to

The United Methodist Church. They are the Articles of Religion of the Church of England and the Confession of Faith of The Evangelical United Brethren Church. They will receive in-depth consideration in Session 4. They represent the basic historical position of The United Methodist Church and are considered to be landmark documents, protected by Articles I and II of Section III of the Constitution from being revoked, altered, or changed by the General Conference.

Basic Tenets of the Protestant Reformation

United Methodism traces many of its doctrinal emphases to the Reformation: the centrality of grace and the life of faith, the authority of Scripture, the sovereignty of God, the priesthood of all believers, the doctrine of calling (vocation), loving God with the mind, and the worship of God.[3]

Grace, as will be seen in subsequent sessions, is central to Protestantism in general and United Methodism in particular. Through Jesus Christ God has expressed the divine grace (John 1:17), which claims human beings, reconciles them to God and one another, and works to transform them into the image of Christ.

The Reformers cried *sola Scriptura* (Scripture alone), as the source and test of faith (*see* Psalm 119:97-105, 111; Luke 24:32; 2 Timothy 3:16). A crucial question for Protestants is, What does the Bible say? The primacy of Scripture in matters of faith continues to be a basic tenet of United Methodism, which puts the church squarely within the Protestant tradition.

The Bible clearly proclaims the sovereignty of God (Genesis 1–2; Job 38–41; Isaiah 40:12-31; Revelation 19:1-2; 21:6). God is free, steadfast, dependable; and to God human beings are accountable. God works in history and shall bring history to fulfillment.

Protestants affirm the priesthood of all believers, which means that each believer is called to be God's representative, one who has authority to communicate and interpret God's will to the people. Priesthood also implies one who intercedes on behalf of the people to God, a mediator of forgiveness. The members of the Christian community are "a holy priesthood"

(1 Peter 2:5). They participate in Christ's ministry by offering themselves to God in service to the world (2 Corinthians 5:18-20).

Protestantism also emphasizes the doctrine of calling, which means that *all* vocations are worthy callings and that Christian vocation can and must be fulfilled, whatever one's "station" in life (Ephesians 4:1). There is no distinction between secular and sacred callings. All of life is the domain of God's purpose and activity, and all persons are called to participate in the divine purpose for the world. Wesley's emphasis on personal and social holiness reflects the Protestant notion that all of life belongs to God. Our affirmation of the ministry of all Christians is an expression of the Protestant belief in the "priesthood of all believers."

Protestantism has emphasized the responsibility of all Christians to love God with the mind (Matthew 22:35-38). *Theology,* which means the study of our knowledge of God, belongs to the whole church, not just to professional clergy. Theology is faith seeking understanding. The responsibility for understanding the faith cannot be relegated to another. Each person must participate in the ongoing theological task. The Wesley emphasis on "practical divinity" and on the role of laypersons in theological formulation reflects its roots in Protestantism.

Protestant worship has distinctive components: the offering of prayer, congregational singing, Scripture and sermon, the offering of gifts, private worship as an extension of public worship. (Compare the scriptural picture of the early church in Acts 2:37-47.) Protestantism also places particular emphasis on the unity of Word and Sacrament. Wesley was steeped in and influenced by *The Book of Common Prayer,* and his heirs have in varying degrees maintained the continuity with the Reformers' practice of worship.

Conclusion

United Methodism began as a movement in the eighteenth century within the broader catholic tradition. However, its roots go deep into the teaching of the Bible and the apostolic church. Perhaps more than any other denomination, United Methodism reflects the variety of theological traditions within the church's history. Although it shares the basic tenets of Protestantism and the Reformed tradition, it carries distinctive marks of Anglicanism and its roots. Since United Methodists share a common heritage with all historic Christian communities, the historic creeds and doctrinal formulations are accepted as gifts that inform and challenge the contemporary church.

THE SESSION PLAN

1. Have on display as people arrive valuable heirlooms, artifacts, and other treasured objects of your local church. These may include Communion ware, paintings, crosses, candlesticks, old Bibles, and a memorial book. Include also copies of the hymnal, the Bible, and *The Book of Worship for Church and Home,* which contains hymns, prayers, and liturgies handed down to us by recent and ancient ancestors.

Call attention first to the objects of the more tangible kind and more recent past. Ask this question: What contribution do these objects make to our life together? (Answers will likely include the following: They remind us of our past, help us recall important persons, decorate our building, help us worship, and so forth.)

After a few minutes of discussion, call attention to the Bible, hymnal, and *Book of Worship.* These contain the oldest gifts to us. Some of the Bible's stories date back four thousand years or more. The hymnal contains hymns that were written hundreds of years ago and psalms composed three thousand years ago. They remind us that we belong to a long tradition. We are surrounded by a great cloud of witnesses (Hebrews 12:1), and we have inherited from the past basic ideas and concepts about God and God's relationship to us. It is humbling and inspiring to realize that we read psalms read by Isaiah and Jeremiah, Jesus and Paul, and that we sing hymns sung by Martin Luther and John Calvin, the Wesleys and Otterbein.

2. Tell the story on page 18 of this leader's guide of the prisoner of war who was sustained by Bible verses, hymns, creeds, and prayers that he remembered. We all have our own functional creeds, or collection of ideas, assump-

tions, and beliefs. They have come to us from many sources in the near or distant past. We have made them our own by relating to them our own experiences and understandings. Ask class members to write down five or six basic ideas, affirmations, phrases, prayers, and so forth that are crucial to them today. You as leader may need to begin by mentioning one of your own to get the group started. (For example, I would list the Great Commandment as one of my basic "creeds.") After allowing three or four minutes for group members to write their statements, you may want to allow some to report affirmations.

Complete this part of the session by saying something like this: "We have just created the elements of a creed. Were we to put our ideas or affirmations into a composite statement, we would have a creed. How would we evaluate its comprehensiveness and accuracy? Partly by comparing it with the historic affirmations of the church. Now let us turn to creeds that we hold in common with other churches."

3. Turn in the hymnal to the creeds (Numbers 880–89 in *The United Methodist Hymnal*). These are among the most precious gifts from our past. Ask this question: Why are they so important? You will want to review for the class the points under "Role and Purpose of Creeds" in this leader's guide. Among the purposes are the following: teaching tools, sources of faith, define boundaries of belief, defense against heresy, means of affirming faith, pledge of loyalty. You as the leader may want to mention that formal creedal statements likely originated as part of the baptism liturgy and therefore were acts of commitment and incorporation into the church. As such they were and are means of fulfilling the church's mission to make disciples of Jesus Christ.

Call attention to the creeds in the hymnal (Numbers 887–89) that are statements from the following Scripture: Romans 8:35, 37-39; 1 Corinthians 15:1-6; Colossians 1:15-20; 1 Timothy 1:15; 2:5-6; 3:16. Ask this question: How do these differ in form and content from the Apostles' Creed and Nicene Creed? (They focus on one central theme or emphasis. They

are biblical quotations rather than statements forged by a council or group.)

4. Focus on the historic creeds by distributing photocopies of the annotated Apostles' Creed and Nicene Creed on pages 23–24 of this leader's guide. Present the brief background of the creeds given in this leader's guide. Have class members read the annotated creeds. Ask them to compare the affirmations that they wrote personally with these creeds. Are their personal affirmations compatible with the historic creeds? What changes, if any, would they like to make in the creeds? Additions? Deletions? Change of language?

5. Call attention to the fact that different branches of the church have, from time to time, felt the need to develop doctrinal statements and creeds. For example, the Heidelberg Catechism was formulated in the sixteenth century in Germany and became a formative summary of the faith for many Protestants in the Reformed tradition. Also, when the Church of England broke with the Roman Catholic Church, the Articles of Religion were adopted as statements of belief in the Church of England. John Wesley provided a revision of those articles for the Methodists. The Confession of Faith of The Evangelical United Brethren Church represents a summary of that church's faith and is now part of United Methodist doctrine. So the theological statement we are studying is part of the continuing work of developing and refining and using our creedal gifts from the past. We will examine in more detail our distinctive United Methodist heritage in Session 4.

6. Explain that as United Methodists we share the rich heritage of our Protestant brothers and sisters. Although we share much in common with the Roman Catholic Church, the special emphases of Protestantism are dominant themes of United Methodist theology. We need to review those themes briefly. Other sessions will deal with distinctive United Methodist emphases related to some of the themes. Mention that Protestantism is often thought of in terms of *protest*, that is, as a protest against

certain beliefs or practices in the Roman Catholic Church. Make the point that Luther, Calvin, and other leaders of the Reformation were making *affirmations* as well as protests. They were affirming certain doctrines that had either received minor emphasis or no emphasis in the church of their day.

List on separate sheets of paper the following seven "Central Protestant Affirmations":
1. centrality of grace and the life of faith
2. the authority of Scripture
3. the sovereignty of God
4. the priesthood of all believers
5. the calling of the Christian person
6. loving God with the mind
7. the worship of God

Divide the class into seven teams, one for each emphasis. Give each team a card with the appropriate Scripture references as given on pages 19–20 of this leader's guide. Ask each team to look up the passage and the doctrine assigned. If you have access to Bible commentaries and dictionaries, those resources will be helpful. As teams reach conclusions regarding their specific doctrine, have a representative write them on chalkboard or posterboard under the appropriate doctrine. After all have finished or time runs short, review the seven areas by using the list on chalkboard or posterboard. Fill in gaps if important information has been omitted.

7. Ask class members to look once more at the card or paper on which they listed important personal affirmations. Invite them to spend a few moments in making changes on the basis of today's session. Emphasize that revisions are ongoing for individuals and the church.

8. Summarize with a statement of your own or by reading aloud the "Conclusion" section on page 20 of this leader's guide.

9. Have members stand and repeat in unison the Apostles' Creed.

OR

9. Close with either your own prayer or the following prayer of the great theologian and churchman of the thirteenth century, Thomas Aquinas:

"Give me, O Lord, a steadfast heart, which no unworthy thought can drag downward; an unconquered heart, which no tribulation can wear out; an upright heart, which no unworthy purpose may tempt aside.

"Bestow upon me also, O Lord my God, understanding to know thee, diligence to seek thee, wisdom to find thee, and a faithfulness that may finally embrace thee; through Jesus Christ our Lord. Amen."[4]

---

[1] From *Loyalty to God: The Apostles' Creed in Life and Liturgy*, by Theodore W. Jennings, Jr. (Abingdon Press, 1992), pp. 12–13.
[2] From *John Wesley's Theology Today*, by Colin W. Williams (Abingdon Press, 1960), pages 28–29.
[3] From *The Spirit of Protestantism*, by Robert McAfee Brown (Oxford University Press, 1961), pages 52–156.
[4] From *The Book of Worship for Church and Home*. Copyright © 1964, 1965, by Board of Publication of The Methodist Church, Inc., page 244.

THE APOSTLES' CREED

based on theological formulas current around A.D. 100, though present form probably appeared in 6th or 7th century

Creator of everything in universe

I believe in God the Father Almighty,
maker of heaven and earth;

And in Jesus Christ his only Son our Lord;

"Anointed One," Messiah (Luke 4:16-21; Mark 8:29)

one to whom we owe allegiance

who was conceived by the Holy Spirit,
born of the Virgin Mary,
suffered under Pontius Pilate,
was crucified, dead, and buried;*

Jesus is both human and divine

Jesus experienced pain and death as we do.

the third day he rose from the dead;

God won! Reason for Christian hope

he ascended into heaven,
and sitteth at the right hand of God
the Father Almighty;
from thence he shall come to judge
the quick and the dead.

Jesus the risen Christ lives with the Eternal God.

The future belongs to God.

the living

I believe in the Holy Spirit,
the holy catholic** church,
the communion of saints,
the forgiveness of sins,
the resurrection of the body,
and the life everlasting. Amen.

The family of all people, past, present, and future, who do God's will.

See 1 Corinthians 15.

Life after death. We don't know what it's like. We trust God in life and death. See Romans 14:8.

* Traditional use includes the words, "He descended into hell."

** means <u>universal</u>

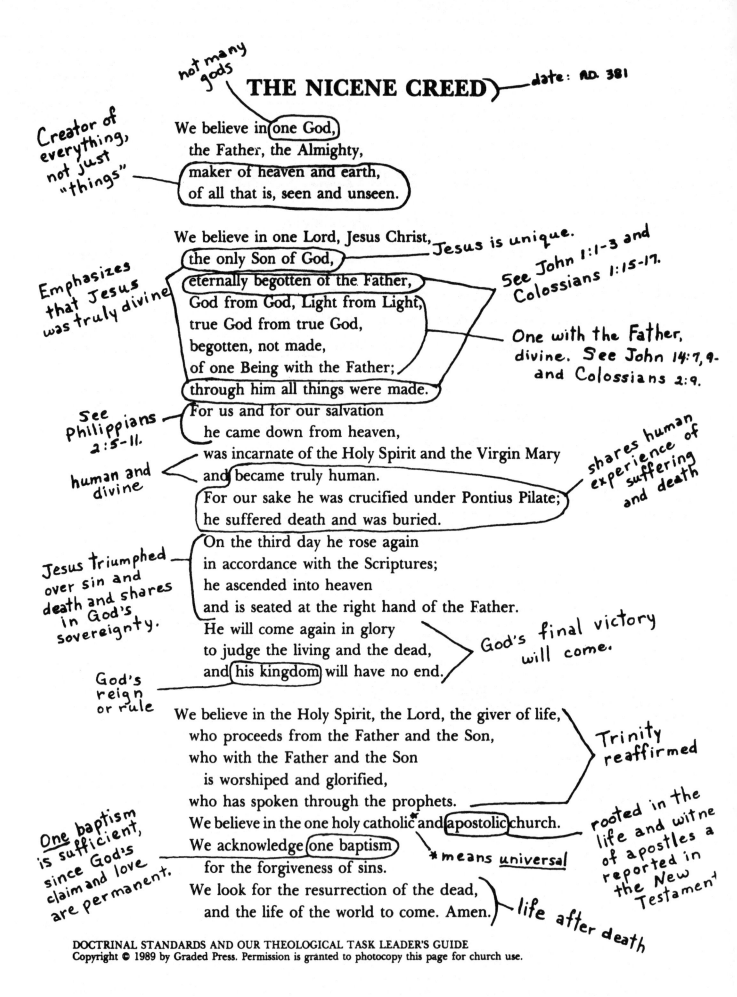

THE NICENE CREED

not many gods

date: A.D. 381

Creator of everything, not just "things"

We believe in one God,
the Father, the Almighty,
maker of heaven and earth,
of all that is, seen and unseen.

We believe in one Lord, Jesus Christ,
the only Son of God,
eternally begotten of the Father,
God from God, Light from Light,
true God from true God,
begotten, not made,
of one Being with the Father;
through him all things were made.

Jesus is unique.

See John 1:1-3 and Colossians 1:15-17.

Emphasizes that Jesus was truly divine

One with the Father, divine. See John 14:7, 9 and Colossians 2:9.

See Philippians 2:5-11.

human and divine

For us and for our salvation
he came down from heaven,
was incarnate of the Holy Spirit and the Virgin Mary
and became truly human.
For our sake he was crucified under Pontius Pilate;
he suffered death and was buried.

shares human experience of suffering and death

Jesus triumphed over sin and death and shares in God's sovereignty.

On the third day he rose again
in accordance with the Scriptures;
he ascended into heaven
and is seated at the right hand of the Father.
He will come again in glory
to judge the living and the dead,
and his kingdom will have no end.

God's final victory will come.

God's reign or rule

We believe in the Holy Spirit, the Lord, the giver of life,
who proceeds from the Father and the Son,
who with the Father and the Son
is worshiped and glorified,
who has spoken through the prophets.

Trinity reaffirmed

We believe in the one holy catholic* and apostolic church.
We acknowledge one baptism
for the forgiveness of sins.

*means universal

rooted in the life and witness of apostles a reported in the New Testament

One baptism is sufficient, since God's claim and love are permanent.

We look for the resurrection of the dead,
and the life of the world to come. Amen.

life after death

WE SHARE THIS FAITH

Purpose of This Session:
To help adults grasp, at least in summary form, the basic affirmations that United Methodists hold in common with all faithful Christians.

Goals of This Session:
1. To help adults become familiar with basic Christian affirmations.
2. To enable participants to recognize and appreciate the core of beliefs that unite Christians.
3. To introduce participants to Wesley's emphasis on *catholic spirit*.

GROUNDING IN SCRIPTURE AND THE *DISCIPLINE*
(Discipline, ¶ 101; student book, pages 7–17)

In order to understand and appreciate our distinctiveness as a denomination, we must first appreciate and celebrate the faith we share with other denominations. Understanding the basic core of faith affirmations prepares us to comprehend more fully and to appreciate more deeply the particular theological emphases of The United Methodist Church. The following sections represent a summary of those beliefs that United Methodists hold in common with other Christians.

The Triune God
Christians share in the affirmations that God is known and experienced as Father, Son, and Holy Spirit. The trinitarian formulation is found in the historic creeds, and, although it is not specifically defined in the New Testament, references are made there to the persons of the Trinity. The disciples are commissioned by the risen Christ to baptize "in the name of the Father and of the Son and of the Holy Spirit" (Matthew 28:19). Paul's letters contain greetings and blessings that reflect the trinitarian imagery (Romans 1:1-7; 1 Corinthians 1:1-3; 2 Corinthians 1:2-3; Philippians 1:2). References to the action of God as Father in creation, as Son in Jesus Christ, and Holy Spirit as a present power run through the New Testament (John 14:16-31; 16:12-15; Acts 2:29-33, 38-39; Romans 5:1-5).

Throughout the church's history various ways of explaining the Trinity have emerged, and the attempt to clarify the concept's meaning and change its language continues. Two intepretations have dominated the church's thinking. One interpretation emphasizes the social or family imagery. Basically, it pictures God as three distinct and separate beings united as one in the way a family is one. The Godhead is three persons, three beings—Father, Son, and Holy Spirit. The three, however, are one in purpose and qualities.

The second theory of the Trinity understands the three persons as three modes of revelation of the one God. God is known as Father (Creator) and speaks through the creation. The same being became incarnate in historic Jesus of Nazareth. Through Jesus Christ, God's anointed, God acted decisively to redeem and reconcile the human family. God is also present as Holy Spirit, one who sustains, guides, and empowers persons and communities. This theory defines *person* in terms of roles God plays. God is "three in one" in the same way a woman may be mother, daughter, and friend.

Neither theory of the Trinity is wholly adequate. The core of the doctrine is this: God cannot be fully contained or expressed in any one category or experience. The doctrine of the Trinity is an attempt to describe the indescribable. Yet God is known in and through the created order. God is known and experienced in the historic Jesus and the risen Christ. God is also known and experienced as a presence that sustains, inspires, guides, and empowers. God, in God's own being and essence, contains unity amid diversity and mystery amid revelation. At the core of God's own being is community bound together and expressed in the power of love.

The current debate in the church over substituting for the traditional language the terms *Creator, Redeemer,* and *Sustainer* raises the issue of God's *essence* versus God's *functions,* or acts. Neither the traditional language nor the proposed substitute fully expresses the meaning of the Trinity.

Two extremes must be avoided if the historic doctrine is to be preserved. On one hand, defenders of the traditional language must avoid reducing the Trinity to its linguistic formulations. That is, God's essence is not fully contained in the words *Father, Son,* and *Holy Spirit.* On the other hand, proponents of changing the language must avoid stripping God of personal attributes and limiting the divine reality to depersonalized actions.

Salvation in and Through Jesus Christ

"We hold in common with all Christians a faith in the mystery of salvation in and through Jesus Christ" (*Discipline,* ¶ 101; student book, page 9); and the church exists to "make disciples of Jesus Christ" (*Discipline,* ¶¶ 120–21; student book, pages 55–56). God has taken the initiative in and through Jesus Christ to restore the divine image in humanity and to bring the whole of creation into harmony with the nature and purposes of God. Two historic claims about Jesus have been in the forefront of Christian thought and belief.

One is that Jesus Christ is the *incarnation* of God's redemptive action. Jesus as the embodiment of God's loving presence and power is affirmed in the Bible and the historic creeds. The stories of Jesus' birth (Matthew 1:18–2:23; Luke 1–2) are the Gospel writers' affirmation that Jesus is the Son of God.

John's Gospel affirms the Incarnation in these memorable words: "The Word became flesh and lived among us, and we have seen his glory, the glory as of a father's only son" (John 1:14). Paul's Letter to the Colossians contains what may be considered a New Testament creed of the Incarnation: "He is the image of the invisible God, the firstborn of all creation; for in him all things in heaven and on earth were created, things visible and invisible. . . . He himself is before all things, and in him all things hold together. . . . For in him all the fullness of God was pleased to dwell, and through him God was pleased to reconcile to himself all things, whether on earth or in heaven, by making peace through the blood of his cross" (Colossians 1:15-20).

The implications of the Word made flesh are many: God is knowable in human experiences. God has claimed all of life as the domain of the divine, from lowly stables to lofty palaces, from cruel crosses to sealed tombs, from teeming marketplaces to peaceful hills. God has identified with human beings and entered into the suffering, vulnerability, and struggle of human beings. Therefore, God understands our plight and feels the pain, alienation, and brokenness of the human family. God has made known the full potential of human beings, for Jesus is the revelation both of God and of God's goal for all persons. Since God in Jesus Christ triumphed over sin and death, the future belongs to God. God has won the decisive victory over all that thwarts God's purpose. Nothing in life or death can separate us from God's love (Romans 8:38-39).

The second historic claim about Jesus in both the Bible and creeds is that he is the means of our *atonement* with God. In the life, death, and resurrection of Jesus the Christ, God did everything necessary to overcome all that separates us from God, from our true selves, and from one another. In Christ we are one with God (atonement). The Gospels affirm that the crucifixion of Jesus was more than the execution of a man (Matthew 27; Mark 15; Luke 23; John 19). Mysteriously Christ died on behalf of human beings (Mark 10:45; 1 Timothy 2:5-6). His death represents God's confrontation of evil, and the Resurrection affirms God's ultimate triumph.

Salvation in and through Jesus Christ was the theme of the early church's preaching (Acts 2:29-36). Paul affirmed the message throughout Asia Minor (Romans 5; 1 Corinthians 1:18-25; 2 Corinthians 5:16-19; Galatians 1:3-4; 2:15-21; 3:23-24; Ephesians 1:7-8; 2:1-8; Philippians 2:5-11; Colossians 1:19-20; 1 Thessalonians 5:9-10). It is the consensus of the New Testament and theology through the ages that salvation is made known and experienced in and through Jesus Christ.

There are several *theories* about how the Atonement is effective, and Christians disagree about which theory is most adequate. Probably none is fully adequate. But Christians agree in affirming the Atonement as a *mystery* to be embraced. The specific imagery of how salvation is wrought in and through Christ may vary, and the reality and experience of salvation may be known and expressed in different ways.

When I was a child, our family attended a church in which the preacher's understanding of the Atonement was vastly different from that which I now hold. He said, "Christ died in your place." Now I know his explanation as the *substitutionary theory of the Atonement*. For that preacher, Christ literally took upon himself the punishment for my sins. Although his knowledge of the historic creed was quite limited, that preacher indelibly etched in my own mind the sense that Christ died for *me*, that God so loved *me* that God was willing to let God's own Son die in my place. My intellectual grasp of that affirmation has changed over the years, but the *experience* made possible through that affirmation remains mysteriously fresh and alive.

God's Love Experienced Through the Holy Spirit

"We share the Christian belief that God's redemptive love is realized in human life by the activity of the Holy Spirit, both in personal experience and in the community of believers" (*Discipline*, ¶ 101; student book, page 9).

How are we to experience God's redemptive love? According to the creeds and the biblical witness, the Holy Spirit works within personal experience and in the life of the Christian community to mediate and make real God's redemptive love. (For the biblical foundation for the work of the Holy Spirit, see the references under "The Triune God," page 25 in this leader's guide.)

John Wesley understood the Holy Spirit as God's personal presence in the heart and will of the believer and in the Spirit-filled community and its sacraments. His emphasis was upon the Christian believer as being "indwelt and led by the Spirit within rather than being possessed by the Spirit as if by some irresistible force."[1] The indwelling Spirit convicts of sin, leads to saving grace, and works within the believer and the Christian community to conform persons to the mind of Christ.

The Holy Spirit, then, is known and experienced as an indwelling presence in the heart of the believer *and* as a presence in the life of the community of believers, the church. Through the liturgy, proclamation, sacraments, and sharing in the fellowship and ministry of the church, the Holy Spirit communicates God's love to individuals and the world.

The Universal Church

"We understand ourselves to be part of Christ's universal church when by adoration, proclamation, and service we become conformed to Christ" (*Discipline*, ¶ 101; student book, page 10). As the body of Christ, the church consists of those whose lives are being transformed into the image of God, those who possess the mind of Christ (Philippians 2:1-11). We are initiated and incorporated into the community of Christ through baptism (Matthew 28:19; Acts 2:38-42), which is a sign of the death to sin and God's cleansing, life-giving grace.

Through Holy Communion, we remember Jesus' death and resurrection and participate in the risen presence of Jesus Christ. Through the presence of the risen Christ and the fellowship of those who share in the sacrament, we are nourished for faithful discipleship in the world.

The church always stands in need of renewal, for it imperfectly confirms to the mind of Christ. As the church, we long for the coming of God's reign in the world. While waiting faithfully for God's final victory, we rejoice in the promise of the everlasting life that conquers death and evil.

The Present and Future Reign of God

"With other Christians we recognize that the reign of God is both a present and future reality" (*Discipline*, ¶ 101; student book, page 10). The kingdom or reign of God is the watchword of Jesus' ministry and teaching. Mark announces the beginning of Jesus' ministry in these words: "Jesus came to Galilee, proclaiming the good news of God, and saying, 'The time is fulfilled, and the kingdom of God has come near; repent, and believe in the good news' " (Mark 1:14-15). Many of his parables begin with "The kingdom of heaven [*kingdom of God*] is like . . ." (Matthew 13:24, 31, 33, 44, 45, 47; 20:1; 22:2; 25:1; Mark 4:26, 30-31).

The kingdom of God, according to the Bible and church tradition, is the realm of God's reign. Wherever God's will is done, the kingdom or reign of God is present. The Lord's prayer contains this parallel petition:

"Your kingdom come.

Your will be done" (Matthew 6:10).

When God's will is done, God's reign comes into the present. The theme of Jesus' preaching and the keynote of his ministry is that God's reign is breaking in upon the world. God is bringing a new world, a world of peace and justice, a world of compassion and hope, a world where God's purposes are fulfilled and God's presence is known.

The reign of God is both a present reality and a future hope. Wherever God's power breaks forth in the world, the Kingdom is present. It was present in Jesus' ministry as good news was brought to the poor and captives were released, as the lame walked, the blind began to see, demons were cast out, storms were calmed, forgiveness was pronounced, life was restored. It is present within our world when persons and communities experience freedom from all forms of bondage, when reconciliation and peace among peoples are experienced, where justice is done, and where wholeness and healing come to God's creation.

Yet the reign of God is only partially and fleetingly present. Its fulfillment is not yet. The kingdom or reign of God is still to come. God's vision for the world and the human family remains only dimly perceived and inadequately

lived, but the church lives in hopeful anticipation of the new heaven and the new earth that will conform to the image of Christ.

The church is the community that is called to live *now* as if God's future had already come. The church is an outpost of God's new creation. As such, the church demonstrates that the reign of God is both personal and social. Jesus said, "The kingdom of God is within you" (Luke 17:21, King James Version). But the reign of God is no private experience for the personal glorification of the individual. God's vision is global and universal. It includes the whole of creation. Therefore, the Christian disciple celebrates the reign of God within his or her own experience but hopes for and works toward the fulfillment of God's purposes for the entire creation.

Authority of Scripture in Matters of Faith

"We share with many Christian communions a recognition of the authority of Scripture in matters of faith" (*Discipline*, ¶ 101; student book, page 10). (A more complete discussion of the meaning and role of Scripture will follow in Session 9.)

The Bible is witness to God's redemptive activity in the world. Churches and individual believers vary in their understanding of the source and meaning of Scripture's authority, although they agree that the Bible plays a central role in matters of faith.

For some, the authority of the Bible is rooted in its verbal, factual inerrancy. Since the Bible is inspired by God, it contains no errors or inconsistencies. Others root the Bible's authority in the power of the Living Word behind the written words. They contend that God inspired the writers but that those writers were fallible, imperfect vehicles of the transcendent Word. The Bible contains the Word of God but in the limited language of human beings.

Perhaps neither position fully captures the significance of holy Scripture's power in faith formation. Whether the Bible is taken literally or figuratively as God's Word, it demands to be taken seriously by all who would know God. Its authority in matters of science and history may be questioned, but its authority in matters of faith has remained firm throughout the church's history.

All Christians share in the responsibility to study, interpret, and share the message of the Bible as they share in the general ministry, fellowship, and mission of the church.

Oneness of the Church

"With other Christians, we declare the essential oneness of the church in Christ Jesus" (*Discipline*, ¶ 101; student book, page 11). No denomination or local church is the body of Christ. The universal church is the body of Christ. Paul's image of the oneness of the church is found in Romans and Corinthians. In Romans 11 Paul uses the analogy of an olive tree, with the church being a branch grafted into the tree. The analogy remains relevant for the contemporary church. The church is a tree, and the various denominations or communions comprise its branches. Each branch possesses unique characteristics, but all of them share a mutual origin in the redemptive love of God and all share in a common mission. The *Discipline* affirms, "We advocate and work for the unity of the Christian church" (*Discipline*, ¶ 124; student book, pages 56–57).

The image of the church as a body is found in both Romans 12 and 1 Corinthians 12. Paul affirms the diversity of gifts that God gives to the church. No gift can be fully employed or appreciated in isolation from many other gifts, any more than one organ of the body can function independently of other organs. The church consists of diverse communions with varying emphases and perspectives. Each needs the other, and together they express the unity made possible by Christ, who binds all things together. (The ecumenical understanding and commitment of United Methodists will be discussed in Session 13.)

Conclusion

John Wesley's own words, in a sermon entitled "The Lord Our Righteousness," serve as both an affirmation of our oneness and a warning to those who resist the essential unity of all Christians: "How dreadful and how innumerable are the contests which have arisen about religion! And not only among the children of this world, among those who knew not what true religion was; but even among the children of God, those who had experienced 'the kingdom of God within them.' . . . How many of these in all ages, instead of joining together against the common enemy, have turned their weapons against each other, and so not only wasted their precious time but hurt one another's spirits, weakened each other's hands, and so hindered the great work of their common Master! How many of the weak have hereby been offended! How many of the 'lame turned out of the way'! How many sinners confirmed in their disregard of all religion, and their contempt of those that profess it!"[2]

THE SESSION PLAN

This session is a quick overview of basic Christian beliefs. The purpose is really twofold—exposure to the core doctrines and the development of a sense of oneness with other Christian communions. Not all of the following suggestions can be used in the session, but they do provide options for you as the leader.

1. Ask group members to call out words and phrases that represent beliefs they think are shared by Christians across denominational lines. Record those ideas on chalkboard or posterboard. Then have group members turn to the section "Basic Christian Affirmations" on student book pages 9–11. Have the group identify any major beliefs listed there that should be added to the list already on chalkboard or posterboard. Finally, invite group members to turn to two contemporary creeds in *The United Methodist Hymnal* that attempt to summarize basic Christian beliefs: "A Statement of Faith of the Korean Methodist Church" (Number 884) and "A Modern Affirmation" (Number 885). Ask these questions: Which of these modern creeds best captures crucial, basic Christian beliefs? What words or ideas would you like to change, if you could?

OR

1. Arrange ahead of time for selected pastors or laypersons of other churches in your com-

munity to form a panel to discuss this question: What are the essential, basic Christian affirmations of your denomination?

Provide panel members, in advance, copies of student book pages 9–11. Ask them to comment on those concepts identified as "Basic Christian Affirmations." Do they disagree with any of them? Allow some time for questions and responses from class members. Inviting guests from other denominations to participate in the class session will add to the depth of the experience.

After the panel discussion, ask this question: If we hold so much in common, why has there been conflicts and even animosity between Christian groups? Discuss the relevance of the statement: "In essentials, unity; in nonessentials, liberty; and in all things, charity" (*Discipline,* ¶ 102; student book, page 18).

2. In this step, group members will explore hymns and canticles that speak of God as *triune.* If you have enough copies of *The United Methodist Hymnal* on hand, let each group member flip through the first two sections under "The Glory of the Triune God" (Numbers 57–152). After a few minutes of browsing, let each person talk about his or her favorite hymn in this section. Point out the diverse ways in which our belief in a triune God has been celebrated in music. If you have only one copy of *The United Methodist Hymnal,* you will need to select a few hymns or canticles ahead of time and copy some of the words on posterboard (for example, Numbers 61, 64, 70, 73, 80, 82, 83, 85, 88, 94, 95, 102, 108). Let the group sing or recite the selected hymns or canticles. Point out the variety of ways that ideas about the Trinity are expressed.

Then review for the group the material in this leader's guide under "The Triune God."

3. To help group members consider why the Incarnation has been seen through the ages as an important clue to Jesus and God, ask this question: What *practical* difference in our lives does the Incarnation make?

Then read aloud the following true story:

A thirty-eight-year-old husband and father of two small children is terminally ill with cancer. He and his wife shared with the pastor their frustration in the way others did not fully understand the depth of their pain and anguish. He said, "There is no way anyone who hasn't been in this situation can really know what we're going through. You and our friends can sympathize and care, but you can't experience what we feel." He is right. The Incarnation, however, affirms that God *does* feel their pain and anguish.

Spend a few minutes discussing other practical implications of the Incarnation. Draw upon the material under "Salvation in and Through Jesus Christ" in this leader's guide.

4. Sometimes fictional stories can help us not only to understand doctrines intellectually but also to *experience* their power and significance.

Walter Wangerin's "Ragman," printed below, portrays and evolves a sense of awe before the mystery of the Atonement. Read it aloud to the group.

I saw a strange sight. I stumbled upon a story most strange, like nothing my life, my street sense, my sly tongue had ever prepared me for.

Hush, child, Hush, now, and I will tell it to you.

Even before the dawn on Friday morning I noticed a young man, handsome and strong, walking the alleys of our City. He was pulling an old cart filled with clothes both bright and new, and he was calling in a clear, tenor voice: "Rags!" Ah, the air was foul and the first light filthy to be crossed by such sweet music.

"Rags! New rags for old! I take your tired rags! Rags!"

"Now, this is a wonder," I thought to myself, for the man stood six-feet-four, and his arms were like tree limbs, hard and muscular, and his eyes flashed intelligence. Could he find no better job than this, to be a ragman in the inner city?

I followed him. My curiosity drove me. And I wasn't disappointed.

Soon the Ragman saw a woman sitting on her back porch. She was sobbing into a handkerchief, sighing and shedding a thousand tears. Her knees and elbows made a sad X. Her shoulders shook. Her heart was breaking.

The Ragman stopped his cart. Quickly, he walked to the woman, stepping around tin cans, dead toys, and Pampers.

"Give me your rag," he said so gently, "and I'll give you another."

He slipped the handkerchief from her eyes. She looked up, and he laid across her palm a linen cloth so clean and new that it shined. She blinked from the gift to the giver.

Then, as he began to pull his cart again, the Ragman did a strange thing: he put her stained handkerchief to his own face; and then *he* began to weep, to sob as grievously as she had done, his shoulders shaking. Yet she was left without a tear.

"This *is* a wonder," I breathed to myself, and I followed the sobbing Ragman like a child who cannot turn away from mystery.

"Rags! Rags! New rags for old!"

In a little while, when the sky showed grey behind the rooftops and I could see the shredded curtains hanging out black windows, the Ragman came upon a girl whose head was wrapped in a bandage, whose eyes were empty. Blood soaked her bandage. A single line of blood ran down her cheek.

Now the tall Ragman loked upon this child with pity, and he drew a lovely yellow bonnet from his cart.

"Give me your rag," he said, tracing his own line on her cheek, "and I'll give you mine."

The child could only gaze at him while he loosened the bandage, removed it, and tied it to his own head. The bonnet he set on hers. And I gasped at what I saw: for with the bandage went the wound! Against his brow it ran a darker, more substantial blood—his own!

"Rags! Rags! I take old rags!" cried the sobbing, bleeding, strong, intelligent Ragman.

The sun hurt both the sky, now, and my eyes; the Ragman seemed more and more to hurry.

"Are you going to work?" he asked a man who leaned against a telephone pole. The man shook his head.

The Ragman pressed him: "Do you have a job?"

"Are you crazy?" sneered the other. He pulled away from the pole, revealing the right sleeve of his jacket—flat, the cuff stuffed into the pocket. He had no arm.

"So," said the Ragman. "Give me your jacket, and I'll give you mine."

Such quiet authority in his voice!

The one-armed man took off his jacket. So did the Ragman—and I trembled at what I saw: for the Ragman's arm stayed in its sleeve, and when the other put it on he had two good arms, thick as tree limbs; but the Ragman had only one.

"Go to work," he said.

After that he found a drunk, lying unconscious beneath an army blanket, an old man, hunched, wizened, and sick. He took that blanket and wrapped it round himself, but for the drunk he left new clothes.

And now I had to run to keep up with the Ragman. Though he was weeping uncontrollably, and bleeding freely at the forehead, pulling his cart with one arm, stumbling for drunkenness, falling again and again, exhausted, old, old, and sick, yet he went with terrible speed. On spider's legs he skittered through the alleys of the City, this mile and the next, until he came to its limits, and then he rushed beyond.

I wept to see the change in this man. I hurt to see his sorrow. And yet I needed to see where he was going in such haste, perhaps to know what drove him so.

The little old Ragman—he came to a landfill. He came to the garbage pits. And then I wanted to help him in what he did, but I hung back, hiding. He climbed a wall. With tormented labor he cleared a little space on that hill. Then he sighed. He lay down. He pillowed his head on a handkerchief and a jacket. He covered his bones with an army blanket. And he died.

Oh, how I cried to witness that death! I slumped into a junked car and wailed and mourned as one who has no hope—because I had come to love the Ragman. Every other face had faded in the wonder of this man, and I cherished him; but he died. I sobbed myself to sleep.

I do not know—how could I know?—that I slept through Friday night and Saturday and its night, too.

But then, on Sunday morning, I was awakened by a violence.

Light—pure, hard, demanding light—slammed against my sour face, and I blinked, and I looked, and I saw the last and the first wonder of all. There was the Ragman, folding the blanket most carefully, a scar on his forehead, but alive! And, besides that, healthy! There was no sign of sorrow nor of age, and all the rags that he had gathered shined for cleanliness.

Well, then I lowered my head and, trembling for all that I had seen, I myself walked up to the Ragman. I told him my name with shame, for I was a sorry figure next to him. Then I took off all my clothes in that place, and I said to him with dear yearning in my voice: "Dress me."

He dressed me. My Lord, he put new rags on me, and I am a wonder beside him. The Ragman, the Ragman, the Christ![3]

After a few moments of silence, ask class members to describe their reactions to the story. What Scripture passages or stories come to mind? (Isaiah 53; the Crucifixion; John 3:16; 2 Corinthians 5:17-21)

Review for the group the material on Atonement in this leader's guide under "Salvation in and Through Jesus Christ."

OR

3–4. In this step, group members will explore hymns and canticles that speak of Jesus Christ as God's *Incarnation* and *Atonement.* If you have enough copies of *The United Methodist Hymnal* on hand, let each group member flip through the sections "The Grace of Jesus Christ" and "Christ's Gracious Life" (Numbers 153–327). After a few minutes of browsing, let each person talk about his or her favorite hymn in these sections. Point out the diverse ways the doctrines of Incarnation and Atonement have been celebrated in music. If you have only one copy of *The United Methodist Hymnal,* select a few hymns or canticles ahead of time and copy some of the words on posterboard. (For Incarnation, you might choose from Numbers 182, 196, 204, 211, and 214; for Atonement you might select from Numbers 165, 172, 282, 286, 287, and 289.) Let the group sing or recite some of the selected hymns or canticles. Point out the variety of ways that these two historic clues to the meaning of Jesus Christ have been expressed in song.

Then review for the group the material in this leader's guide under "Salvation in and Through Jesus Christ."

5. Close with the following trinitarian blessing: "The grace of the Lord Jesus Christ, the love of God the Father, and the fellowship of the Holy Spirit bless, abide, and keep you, both now and forever more. Amen."

---

[1] From *The Works of John Wesley, Volume I,* edited by Albert C. Outler (Abingdon Press, 1984), page 75.

[2] From *The Works of John Wesley, Volume I,* page 449.

[3] "Ragman" from *Ragman and Other Cries of Faith,* by Walter Wangerin, Jr. Copyright © 1984 by Walter Wangerin, Jr. Reprinted by permission of Harper & Row, Publishers, Inc.

OUR DISTINCTIVE HERITAGE

Purpose of This Session:
To introduce adults to the foundational theological documents peculiar to United Methodism.

Goals of This Session:
1. To provide information to class members about how the life experiences of Wesley, Otterbein, and Albright helped to shape the theology of The United Methodist Church.
2. To introduce adults to the history and basic content of key documents—the Articles of Religion and the Confession of Faith.
3. To help participants see that the theological documents of our heritage are grounded in Scripture.
4. To help adults understand the role that the foundation documents play in United Methodism's past and present.

GROUNDING IN SCRIPTURE

The basic foundation documents of United Methodism are, in one sense, attempts to summarize the basic message of the Bible. They clearly affirm the centrality of Scripture, and the various affirmations have been tested by the criterion of Scripture. As the primary witness to God's revelation in creation, in history, and supremely in Jesus Christ, the Bible contains important stories that shape what the church believes. The Articles of Religion of The Methodist Church and the Confession of Faith of The Evangelical United Brethren Church attempt to bring together central affirmations of the biblical stories. They owe their existence to the Scripture, and they continue to be evaluated in light of the biblical message.

Specific biblical references in this session will be included in the discussion of the Articles and the Confession. It is important to note that the Bible itself contains summary statements that serve as creeds (refer to Session 2). Therefore, the practice of formulating and establishing doctrinal positions is itself rooted in Scripture. In that way, Scripture models for the church the ongoing theological task.

Wesley's *Sermons on Several Occasions* are "biblical sermons." The themes emerge from Scripture, and the sermons contain generous illustrations from the Bible. Wesley's immersion in the Bible's stories, images, and language is evident in the content and style of his sermons.

Wesley's *Explanatory Notes Upon the New Testament* reflect the grounding of the early Methodists in Scripture. The *Notes* are commentaries and expositions of Scripture that Wesley provided as resources for faith formation and theological inquiry. Since he considered Scripture the primary source and criterion, all other doctrinal and theological statements were attempts to clarify, summarize, or apply the biblical foundation of faith.

WHAT THE *DISCIPLINE* SAYS
(*Discipline*, ¶¶ 102–103;
student book, pages 17–42)

As the historic ecumenical creeds comprise a corpus of belief for all Christians and the basic tenets of Protestantism help to define a broad spectrum of Christendom, the Articles of Religion of The Methodist Church and the Confessions of Faith of The Evangelical United Brethren Church form a "marrow" of doctrine for United Methodists. They, along with

Wesley's *Sermons on Several Occasions* and *Explanatory Notes Upon the New Testament,* are "standards" of doctrine for United Methodists.

United Methodists are "very much aware . . . that God's eternal Word never has been, nor can be, exhaustively expressed in any single form of words" (*Discipline,* ¶ 102; student book, page 17). While we reaffirm the ancient creeds and confessions as valid summaries of the faith, those creeds and confessions are not considered to be doctrinal absolutes. The Articles of Religion and the Confession of Faith are foundational for United Methodists, but they are open to interpretation as they are applied to contemporary realities and continue to be examined in light of Scripture, tradition, reason, and experience.

Wesley's Experience

Doctrinal formulations in the United Methodist tradition were influenced by the life experiences of the early leaders of the movement. In particular, the experiences of Wesley, Otterbein, and Albright were formative of the theological direction of the movements they launched.

John Wesley was born into a home in which vital piety played a dominant role. His father was a priest in the Church of England whose devotion and piety were equaled or exceeded by that of his wife, Susanna. Well educated by his mother, at Charter House School in London, and at Oxford, John Wesley was familiar with the great books and ideas of the world.

While at Oxford as a student and teacher, Wesley became part of the "Holy Club," a small group of students who met daily for prayer and Bible study. They also engaged in social service, such as tutoring children, aiding the poor, and visiting prisons. They sought to be faithful and obedient to God in every moment and in every act.

Wesley spent a brief time in America as a missionary to the colonists and Native Americans in southern Georgia. There he failed miserably. It was there, however, that he was attracted to the Moravians and their emphasis on inner assurance of salvation. Such assurance was an experience he desired but that eluded him. No amount of study or discipline or good works brought him the inner peace he sought.

He returned to England, arriving February 1, 1738. He met with the Moravians regularly and continued his intellectual, spiritual, and social pursuits. He recorded in his journal, May 24, 1738, that during a Society meeting at Aldersgate Street he felt his "heart strangely warmed." He said that the assurance of salvation came to him as he trusted in God alone for his salvation. Although he seldom referred to the experience, it helped to focus a central theme of his preaching and teaching—salvation by grace. One year later, he reluctantly agreed to follow George Whitefield in the practice of "field preaching." He went across England preaching the good news of God's grace and establishing class meetings and societies for the purpose of nurturing persons in the faith. He identified with the poor, and they became his friends and coworkers. He considered regular and ongoing relationship with the poor as indispensable to Christian discipleship as public and private worship and sharing in the sacraments.

Wesley never reduced theology to a confessional formula or doctrine test. He maintained that the basic doctrines in the Anglican Thirty-Nine Articles, the Homilies, and The Book of Common Prayer were adequate. As the movement grew, Wesley provided his people with written sermons and a Bible commentary. His *Sermons on Several Occasions* (1746–60) set forth the doctrines that he embraced and taught as essentials of true religion. His *Explanatory Notes Upon the New Testament* was published in 1755 as a guide for Methodists in biblical and doctrinal interpretation.

When the Methodist movement in America became a church in 1784, Wesley furnished the American Methodists with a liturgy and a doctrinal statement. The doctrinal statement consisted of the Articles of Religion, which was a revision of the Thirty-Nine Articles of the Church of England. The articles had been standards of preaching within the Methodist movement, and in North America they became basic norms for Christian belief within the new church. But the *Sermons* and *Notes* continued to be the traditional standard explanations of Methodist teaching.

The Experience of Otterbein and Albright[1]

Phillip William Otterbein (his family called him William) was born in 1726 in Germany, one of ten children. His father was a school principal and later became the pastor of two Reformed churches. Six sons and one daughter of the ten Otterbein children reached maturity. All six sons became German Reformed ministers, and their sister married a minister.

William Otterbein studied theology at Herborn Academy. There he was exposed to the doctrine of two covenants, the covenant of works and the covenant of grace. The doctrine holds that persons have the responsibility to choose to be subject to one covenant or the other. Otterbein absorbed the influence of Calvinist thought as expressed in the Heidelberg Catechism, the doctrine of the two covenants, and the depth of religious feeling and moral rectitude of pietism.

Otterbein arrived in America in July 1752. The evangelical and pietistic spirit of his earlier ministry was intensified in 1754 while he was the pastor at Lancaster, Pennsylvania. One Sunday after he had preached on the theme of God's grace, a member of the congregation questioned him about the meaning of grace. Otterbein answered, "Advice is scarce with me this day," and he abruptly felt that he lacked vital inner assurance. He went into a quiet room, where after fervent prayer he experienced the inner assurance. He preached with new power and conviction and eventually formed the United Brethren in Christ.

Jacob Albright, founder of the Evangelical Movement, was born in 1759 and reared in a German-speaking family. In 1790, several of his six children died in an epidemic of dysentery. Albright wondered whether their deaths were punishment for his indifference to the religious life. He consulted three devout men: Anthony Houtz, an evangelically minded German Reformed minister who had conducted the funeral of the children; Isaac Davies (or Davis), a Methodist lay preacher who farmed nearby; and Adam Riegel, another neighbor and an associate of Otterbein and Martin Boehm.

In the summer of 1791, Albright attended a prayer meeting in Riegel's home. He poured out his soul to those present and to God. He is quoted as testifying, "All fear and anxiety of heart disappeared. Joy and blessed peace inbreathed my breast. God gave witness to my spirit that I had become a child of God."[2]

Albright joined a Methodist class and reluctantly accepted a call to the ministry in 1796. He too began to form classes after the fashion of the Methodist class to which he had belonged. He gradually, however, allowed his Methodist affiliation, including his exhorter's license, to lapse. He later formed The Evangelical Association.

Wesley, Otterbein, and Albright shared a basic emphasis on conversion, justification by faith, Christian nurture, the priesthood of all believers, and sanctification as the goal of Christian life. They also stressed Scripture as the primary source and norm for Christian teaching and preaching.

The current Confession of Faith of The Evangelical United Brethren Church represents the culmination of revisions and refinement over a period of about 150 years. It reflects the influence of the Methodists, The Evangelical Association of Albright, Otterbein's United Brethren in Christ, the Heidelberg Catechism, and the Augsburg Confession. The union with The Methodist Church in 1968 brought together the Articles of Religion and the Confession of Faith as doctrinal standards for The United Methodist Church.

Doctrinal Standards and the Restrictive Rules

The Plan of Union for The United Methodist Church accepts the Methodist Articles of Religion, the Evangelical United Brethren Confession of Faith, and Wesley's *Sermons* and *Notes* as established standards of doctrine.

The Constitution of The United Methodist Church, in its Restrictive Rules (*Discipline*, ¶¶ 16–20), protects both the Articles of Religion and the Confession of Faith as doctrinal standards that are not to be revoked, altered, or changed.

On the surface, it would appear that the Restrictive Rules move The United Methodist Church in the direction of a more narrowly defined and less flexible doctrinal position. Two factors, however, prevent United

Methodism from becoming a doctrinally rigid church. One is the tradition, preserved in the current theological statement, emphasizing practical divinity. Second, the inclusion of Wesley's *Sermons* and *Notes* as additional standards makes rigidity in doctrine less likely. It is important to remember that when Methodist preachers and leaders asked Wesley for help in doctrinal matters, he did not give them creeds. He gave them sermons and a commentary on the New Testament. Thereby, the standards for doctrine were more open and flexible, with the final standard being Scripture.

The Articles of Religion and the Confession of Faith, then, are not dogmatic creeds that allow no variation in interpretation. They are parameters and guidelines that themselves require continuing theological inquiry and exploration. They are part of the foundation of the United Methodist theological structure. They are not its ceiling.

The Articles of Religion and the Confession of Faith

The twenty-five Articles of Religion and the sixteen articles of the Confession of Faith fall into twelve major affirmations. The following represents a brief description of the basic beliefs of the documents, along with their biblical foundation.

The Trinity (Article I and Confession I). Both documents clearly affirm the historical doctrine of the triune God. The doctrine affirms at least these truths about God: (1) God is mystery and cannot be totally captured by any categories. (2) God is relational and is known in relationships. (3) Within the being of God there is unity amid diversity. (4) God is known and experienced in creation; in the life, teachings, death, and resurrection of Jesus Christ; and in a Presence that comforts, confronts, challenges, guides, and sustains us.

The basic foundation for the doctrine of the Trinity is laid in Scripture. Scripture makes no arguments for God's existence. In both the Old and New Testaments, God's existence is assumed and God chooses to reveal God's self. In the Old Testament God is described as a living God (Jeremiah 10:10), as one (Deuteronomy 6:4), as Creator (Genesis 1–2;

Nehemiah 9;6), and as holy other (Isaiah 6:3). In the New Testament, God is described as Father and Jesus as Son (Matthew 26:39; John 14:8-11, 20, 28; 1 Corinthians 8:6; James 2:19). Jesus is described as the Son of God (Matthew 16:16), judge (Matthew 25:31-33), and mediator (Colossians 1:16-20; Hebrews 1:1-4).

"The Spirit of God" was active in Creation (Genesis 1:2, Revised Standard Version). The Spirit guides and inspires kings, priests, and prophets. Jesus promises that he will send the Spirit (Counselor) to be with his followers forever (John 14:26; 15:26; 20:22). God's Spirit is related to the Son and seeks to redeem (Galatians 4:4-6).

Jesus Christ, the Word Made Flesh (Article II and Confession II). These articles proclaim that Jesus is the supreme expression of God's nature and God's intention for human beings. Jesus was fully human and experienced the full range of human temptation, anguish, suffering, and death. Yet he was also fully divine, one with God. His sacrificial death overcomes sin and reconciles humanity to God. Jesus Christ is the Lord of the future who intercedes on our behalf and by whom all humanity will be judged.

The Gospels support these articles in their proclamation of the identity and work of Jesus Christ. John proclaims Jesus as the Word made flesh (John 1:1, 14). The virgin birth is one means of affirming that Jesus is both human and divine (Matthew 1:18-25; Luke 1:30-35). Christ is described as mediator (1 Timothy 2:5), as the pioneer of salvation (Hebrews 2:10), and as the perfecter of faith (Hebrews 12:2). In him "all the fullness of God was pleased to dwell" (Colossians 1:19), and through him God has reconciled humanity to God and brought a new creation into being (2 Corinthians 5:14-20).

The Resurrection (Article III and Confession XII). The basic theme of the early church's preaching was "Jesus Christ is risen from the dead." It has been a central message throughout the church's history. Christ has triumphed over sin and death. God in Christ has taken all the evil and suffering and death that the world can give and has been victorious. The resurrection of Jesus Christ is God's eternal *no* to evil and death and God's everlasting *yes* to everything Jesus was, everything he said, and everything he did. Because sin and death have been conquered, we can share in the victory. We can trust God with even our own death.

The New Testament contains five different accounts of the Resurrection (Matthew 28:1-10; Mark 16:1-8; Luke 24:1-49; John 20:1-21; 1 Corinthians 15:3-8). In addition, several sermons refer to the Resurrection (Acts 2:29-36; 3:12-26; 7:2-53; 13:16-41; 17:22-31; 21:27–22:21). The New Testament agrees that the resurrection of Jesus was God's act (Acts 2:24, 32; Romans 6:4; 1 Corinthians 15:15). A new age has been inaugurated, and we can await with confidence our sharing in the Resurrection (1 Corinthians 15).

The Holy Spirit (Article IV and Confession III). (Refer to the material in the section on the Trinity for a fuller discussion and biblical references.) According to the New Testament, the Holy Spirit is the power of God in the church (John 14–16). The Spirit brought the church into being at Pentecost (Acts 2:1-21) and endows the community with gifts, especially the gift of love (1 Corinthians 12–13). The believer shares in the life of God's Spirit in the church (Ephesians 3:20-21). The Holy Spirit continues to renew the church, leads persons to salvation, and assures persons of God's reconciling love.

The Sufficiency of Scripture for Salvation (Articles V, VI, and Confession IV). The role of Scripture in matters of faith is discussed in Sessions 2, 3, and 9. These articles clearly identify Scripture as the central, primary source and criterion of doctrine and theology.

Article VI affirms the continuity between the Old and New Testaments. It reveals God's mighty acts and God's covenant, and it prepares for God's revelation in Jesus the Christ. Although the ceremonial and ritualistic laws of the Old Testament are not binding on the Christian, "no Christian whatsoever is free from the obedience of the commandments which are called moral."

Sin and Free Will (Articles VII, VIII, and Confession VII). The understanding of human sin receives additional consideration in Session 5.

Someone has remarked that the only Christian doctrine for which there is irrefutable, empirical evidence is the doctrine of original sin. These articles clearly affirm the depth and power of human sin and the futility of human efforts alone to triumph over it. Original sin means that human beings, before they are conscious of choosing good and evil, have already become so immersed in and bound by sin that they naturally are inclined to evil. Whether the essence of sin is seen as pride, as the refusal to accept one's humanness and God's sovereignty, as the betrayal of the divine image, or as missing the mark of God's goal for the human family, the Bible and historical theology bear witness to its insidious and systemic nature.

According to the Bible, sin is rooted in the human refusal to live in loving and obedient relationship with God. It is the refusal of God's vision for the world and human life (Genesis 3; Psalms 14:2-3; 51:5; Jeremiah 17:9). Paul described the power of sin in these memorable words: "I can will what is right, but I cannot do it. For I do not do the good I want, but the evil I do not want is what I do. Now if I do what I do not want, it is no longer I that do it, but sin that dwells within me" (Romans 7:18-20). He expressed the true condition of the human family when he cried out, "Who will rescue me from this body of death?" (7:24).

Justification by Faith (Articles IX, XII, and Confession IX). A fuller treatment of justification and grace is to be found in Session 5.

These articles, in keeping with the biblical witness, assert that God takes the initiative to conquer sin and reconcile the human family. In spite of our sin, we are made right with God by God's own unmerited love. That which we cannot do for ourselves, God does on our behalf.

Wesley felt it necessary to include an article regarding sin after justification (Article XII). He contended that justification does not prevent further sin and that sin after justification is pardonable. We can turn away from the grace given us, but God always stands ready to welcome us when we repent.

Paul highlighted the biblical understanding of justification by faith in his Letter to the Romans. He wrote, "Therefore, since we are justified by faith, we have peace with God through our Lord Jesus Christ" (Romans 5:1). Through Christ, we have been reconciled to God (2 Corinthians 5:17-19), who died for us while we were yet sinners (Romans 5:8).

Good Works, Sanctification, and Perfection (Articles X, XI, and Confession X, XI). The relationship between faith and works receives additional consideration in Session 6.

Good works are responses to God's grace, not attempts to earn God's favor. Growth in grace is an endless process of growth toward becoming perfect in love. God's grace is capable of removing from us the desire to sin and enabling us to be holy as God is holy. It is impossible, however, for us to render unto God more than is required (works of supererogation). However faithful we may be, we can never do enough to boast of having earned God's grace.

The entire biblical record is a call to faithfulness and obedience in response to God's gracious acts of deliverance and redemption. From the giving of the Law (Exodus 20:1-20) to Jesus' call to "Follow me" (Matthew 4:19), God calls human beings to active participation in the reign of God. And no amount of faith makes works unnecessary (James 2:18-26).

The Church (Article XIII, Confession V). The doctrine of the church receives considerable discussion in Sessions 1 and 13. An extensive listing of the biblical images of the church is found in Session 1.

The church is a community of believers who respond to the lordship of Christ. Through the proclamation of the Word and the administration of the sacraments, the Holy Spirit works to redeem and nurture followers of Christ. The church in its worship, fellowship, and service is an outpost of God's reign in the world.

The Sacraments (Articles XVI, XVII, XVIII, XIX, and Confession VI). United Methodists acknowledge and participate in two sacraments, the Lord's Supper and baptism. *Sacraments* has come to mean the special rites or ceremonies that are commanded in the New Testament by Christ and that portray the depth of the gospel.

Jesus directed the disciples to make disciples of all nations, "baptizing them in the name of the Father and of the Son and of the Holy Spirit" (Matthew 28:18-20). Baptism is the sign of God's grace in cleansing, forgiving, and renewing. Through baptism persons are marked as Christian disciples and initiated into the fellowship of believers. Since baptism is a sign of God's grace, not the sign of human effort or response, infants and children are baptized.

Jesus also commanded the disciples to share in a meal in which the bread and wine became signs of his broken body and shed blood (Matthew 26:26-29; Mark 14:22-25; Luke 22:17-20; 1 Corinthians 11:23-26). Through the Lord's Supper (Holy Communion, the Eucharist), we remember God's action in Christ. It is also a celebration of our relationship to the living Christ and a renewal of our covenant with God.

Relationship to Rulers and Government (Articles XXIII, XXV, and Confession XVI). Article XXIII reflects the Methodists' support of the American government as formed by the Constitution. This article was approved by the Christmas Conference of 1784. A note was added in 1939 that sought to interpret the article by calling all Christians in all lands to respect the authority of government. Article XXV acknowledges the validity of giving one's oath in testimony before magistrates and legal officials. Article XVI is more inclusive in its statement regarding civic responsibility. It affirms the responsibility of governments to protect "human rights under God," and it rejects war and bloodshed as contrary to the gospel. Citizens are "to give moral strength and purpose to their respective governments through sober, righteous and godly living."

The key biblical foundation for the Christian's responsibility to civil authority is Romans 13:1-7. Paul called upon the Roman Christians to be subject to the rulers. Jesus acknowledged the authority of the state in his statement regarding taxes (Matthew 22:15-22).

Lest the state be considered sovereign, however, it must be remembered that Scripture permits no sovereign but God. Furthermore, Paul, who affirmed the role of civil authority, was executed by civil authority. When brought before authorities, Peter and the apostles said, "We must obey God rather than any human authority" (Acts 5:29; *see also* 4:19-20).

Public Worship and Rites and Ceremonies (Article XV, XXII, and Confession XIII, XIV). The Confession of Faith explicitly affirms that public worship is an essential duty and privilege. It allows for diversity in forms of worship and calls for it to be done in a language and form understood by the people. The Confession further acknowledges the importance of "the Lord's Day" as "divinely ordained for private and public worship, for rest from unnecessary work, and should be devoted to spiritual improvement, Christian fellowship and service."

The Articles of Religion acknowledge that different contexts and circumstances call for varied rites and ceremonies (Article XXII) and that public worship should be in a language understood by the people (Article XV).

Worship of God is the natural response of people to God. The Psalms reflect the worship of the people of Israel, and they persistently call the community to prayer and praise. Jesus regularly participated in worship in the Temple and synagogue (Luke 4:16). The early church gathered on Sunday as a commemoration of the Resurrection, and worship was a vital part of their life together as a community.

Other Articles have to do with permitting the marriage of ministers (Article XXI), rejection of the idea of purgatory (Article XIV), and belief in righteous judgment as a present and future reality (Confession XII). Article XXIV and Confession XV deal with stewardship of property. They acknowledge that God is the owner of all things and that the Christian has the responsibility to use property in a manner that manifests love and liberality.

Wesley's *Sermons* and *Notes*

In addition to the Articles of Religion and the Confession of Faith. Wesley's *Sermons on Several Occasions* and *Explanatory Notes Upon the New Testament* are foundation documents for United Methodist doctrine and theology.

Wesley considered *Sermons on Several Occasions* as definitive of his role as preacher, teacher, evangelist, and pastor. The eight volumes cover more than forty years of Wesley's preaching.

They contain his basic understanding of the faith and its implications for persons and society. According to Albert C. Outler, Wesley's written sermons were specifically for the purpose of nurture and reflection, while his oral sermons were for proclamation and invitation. His *Sermons on Several Occasions,* then, sought to instruct the Methodists on the basic tenets of the faith.

It is important to note that the *Sermons* as standards of doctrine, allow for flexibility in doctrinal development and theological inquiry. Since Wesley continued to add to the collection new sermons on emerging topics, he obviously saw the work of theology as ongoing and dynamic. Since the sermons reflect Wesley's own development in thought and experience, there is diversity of viewpoint within the sermons. Consequently, as standards, the sermons allow for some flexibility and continuing development.

Explanatory Notes Upon the New Testsament was provided to the Methodists as a tool for interpreting the Bible. Some of Wesley's notes on the biblical passages were original, but some ideas he borrowed from other commentaries that he had found useful. Wesley considered the *Notes* and *Sermons* as containing the basic parameters of sound doctrine. Therefore, they have become foundation documents for United Methodist doctrine and theology. Their expansiveness and flexibility provide United Methodists with guidelines and boundaries while encouraging openness and continued theological inquiry.

Conclusion

United Methodism, while sharing kinship with all Christian communities, contributes a unique heritage to the broader Christian community. The experiences of Wesley, Otterbein, Albright, and other early leaders helped to forge the foundation documents of our heritage. The Articles of Religion, the Confession of Faith, and Wesley's *Sermons* and *Notes* form a solid foundation upon which United Methodism's theological identity is built. While identifying basic tenets of the faith, they allow for and require continuing reflection, interpretation, and amplification. They are gifts that invite us to discover who we are. And they are tools by which our identity is expanded and enriched.

THE SESSION PLAN

1. Begin with a brief review of the last session. You may want to say something like this: "We as United Methodists are members of a larger family of Christians. As members of that larger family, we have been given gifts that help us to know who we are. Those gifts also provide the foundation upon which we expand our identity. The gifts are creeds and affirmations. The Apostles' Creed and Nicene Creed and the basic affirmations of Protestantism help to define who we are."

2. Explain that, as United Methodists, we are a nuclear family within the extended family. Ask class members to go through their wallets or purses and select objects or documents that help to identify them as unique individuals and families. Likely means of identification will include driver's license, social security card, credit cards, and photographs. Others may be more personal, related to past experiences or associations. For example, "I have in my billfold a 'Life Membership in The Methodist Men.' It was given to me when I was eighteen by the club in the small rural church in which I grew up. Most of the men who were members at that time have died. The card reminds me of my spiritual roots and many of the persons who nurtured me in the faith."

Ask members to describe to the class the item(s) that they consider most important in defining who they are.

3. Call attention to the four foundation documents that define our United Methodist family identity: Articles of Religion, Confession of Faith, *Sermons on Several Occasions,* and *Explanatory Notes Upon the New Testament.* Remind the class that the documents serve three basic purposes: (1) to identify core beliefs, (2) to establish guidelines and parameters, and (3) to challenge and nurture growth in faith and understanding.

4. Remind the class that United Methodist beliefs and affirmations grow out of life concerns, not out of abstract speculations about doctrines and beliefs. Behind these foundation documents are *persons* whose particular life experiences were the seedbed from which the documents emerged.

Present an account of the experiences of Wesley, Otterbein, and Albright in one of the following ways: Assign ahead of time to three class members the responsibility to summarize briefly the faith journeys of the three forebears. *John Wesley, His Life and Theology,* by Robert G. Tuttle; *John Wesley,* by Stanley Ayling; and *The Elusive Mr. Wesley,* by Richard Heitzenrater, are potential resources. A concise sketch of Otterbein and Albright may be found in *The History of the Evangelical United Brethren Church,* by J. Bruce Behney and Paul H. Eller. Or, distribute to class members copies of the material on the three in this leader's guide.

After hearing or reading the summaries, ask these questions: How were their experiences similar? (Answers: sense of assurance, use of small groups for nurture, experience of assurance after period of struggle and turmoil, Wesley and Otterbein deeply religious prior to their sense of assurance, became leaders of movements.) In what ways were their beliefs shaped by their life experiences? (Answers: Wesley and Otterbein had sought peace through obedience and diligence but came to emphasize grace as a source of peace. Albright, Otterbein, and Wesley had been part of small groups such as the Holy Club and class meetings. They all were disciplined persons.)

5. Ask class members to recall their personal affirmations from the previous session. How were those affirmations influenced by their experiences? Invite members to describe their feelings. If they do not share, simply state that most of us emphasize particular aspects of Christian belief because of our experiences.

6. Review the Articles and the Confession by following the grouping in this leader's guide. Put the article numbers from the Articles of Religion and the Confession of Faith in each group at the top of a sheet of paper. On each

sheet list the biblical references cited in this guide. Distribute the sheets to class members. Since there will be twelve to fourteen sheets, persons will work individually or in small teams, depending on the size of the class. Have the individuals or small teams write the following information on the sheet of paper: a one-sentence summary or paraphrase of the articles assigned, a statement of the biblical foundation, and questions they have about the articles. Allow a good bit of time for the work to be done. Then ask each person or team to report what is on the sheet to the whole group. As persons or teams report information, tape the sheets to a wall where others may see them after the session. Respond to questions as they arise.

7. Refer to Wesley's *Sermons on Several Occasions* and *Explanatory Notes Upon the New Testament*. Explain that *Sermons* consists of eight volumes developed over more than forty years. The sermons cover the range of Wesley's teachings and beliefs, as does the commentary in *Notes*. If you have the volumes of both in your church library, bring them to class. Pass them around the room. Invite persons to browse through them while you make the point that they provide a foundation of belief, establish boundaries of doctrine, and allow flexibility and growth in theological inquiry.

8. Before the class session, find copies of two sermons by Wesley, which are included in *Sermons on Several Occasions:* "Catholic Spirit" and "Salvation by Faith." Present the content of these sermons to the class, perhaps reading excerpts aloud as examples of foundation documents and as preparation for succeeding sessions.

9. Read together as an affirmation of faith Article IX of the Confession of Faith, "Justification and Regeneration."

10. Close with an extemporaneous prayer, or use the following prayer from the Covenant Service, which was first used in 1755 and is found in *The Book of Worship for Church and Home*:

I am no longer my own, but thine. Put me to what thou wilt, rank me with whom thou wilt; put me to doing, put me to suffering; let me be employed for thee or laid aside for thee, exalted for thee or brought low for thee; let me be full, let me be empty; let me have all things, let me have nothing; I freely and heartily yield all things to thy pleasure and disposal.

And now, O glorious and blessed God, Father, Son, and Holy Spirit, thou art mine, and I am thine. So be it. And the covenant which I have made on earth, let it be ratified in heaven. Amen.[3]

---

[1]Information about Otterbein and Albright from *The History of the Evangelical United Brethren Church, The History of the Evangelical United Brethren Church*, by J. Bruce Behney and Paul H. Eller (Abingdon Press, 1979).

[2] From *The History of the Evangelical United Brethren Church*, page 69.

[3] From *The Book of Worship for Church and Home* (Copyright © 1964, 1965 by Board of Publication of The Methodist Church, Inc.) page 387.

AN EMPHASIS ON GRACE

Purpose of This Session:
To help adults grasp Wesley's threefold understanding of grace and consider what God's grace does and could mean for their own lives.

Goals of This Session:
1. To show the relevance of grace in today's world.
2. To identify key biblical foundations for understanding the nature of sin and salvation through grace.
3. To enable participants to understand Wesley's concept of prevenient, justifying, and sanctifying grace.
4. To invite participants to open their lives to God's gracious love.

GROUNDING IN SCRIPTURE

Four stories in Genesis portray the origin and nature of sin:
• Adam and Eve (Genesis 3)
• Cain and Abel (4:1-24)
• the Flood (6–9)
• the tower of Babel (11:1-9)

According to these four passages, sin originated in human pride, which results in the refusal to accept limitations. Adam and Eve resisted God's prohibition against eating of the tree of the knowledge of good and evil. The subtle promise of the Tempter was, "When you eat of it [*the tree*] . . . you will be like God, knowing good and evil" (Genesis 3:5). That is, you will know everything. The confusing of freedom with total independence and the desire to be all-knowing and all-powerful cause us to be alienated from one another, from the earth itself, and from God.

Cain's jealousy of his brother, Abel was rooted in his unwillingness to accept God's claim. God refused Cain's offering while accepting Abel's. Instead of acknowledging God's right to make such a choice, Cain rebelled against it and struck out against his brother, whom he considered to be a threat to his position with the Almighty.

The sin of the whole human race is illustrated in the presumptuousness of this claim in Genesis 6:4-5: "The sons of God went in to the daughters of humans, who bore children to them. . . . The LORD saw that the wickedness of humankind was great in the earth, and that every inclination of the thoughts of their hearts was only evil continually." The line between God and human creatures had been so blurred that human creatures thought they were God and could even give birth to God's offspring.

"Come, let us build ourselves a city, and a tower with its top in the heavens, and let us make a name for ourselves" (Genesis 11:4). Again, the essence of sin lies in discontent with being human and wanting to be God. Such pride creates division, competitiveness, and an inability to communicate.

Human beings are sinners! The New Testament affirms, "All have sinned and fall short of the glory of God" (Romans 3:23), and "If we say that we have no sin, we deceive ourselves, and the truth is not in us" (1 John 1:8). Sin is to fall short of God's intention for us. It is to miss the mark. Sin has power over us as drugs have a hold on an addict. We are addicted to sin—to pride, self-promotion, the failure to fulfill the divine image, and the refusal to accept our creatureliness.

Yet the last word is not human sin. It is divine

grace. The final word to Adam and Eve was not punishment, for "the LORD God made garments of skins for the man and for his wife, and clothed them" (Genesis 3:21).

As an act of divine mercy, God placed "a mark on Cain, so that no one who came upon him would kill him" (4:15). Cain was given a new future, another chance to be who he was created to be.

The rainbow after the Flood signaled a new tomorrow for Noah and his family, and God entered into a covenant of promise with the people (9:8-13). The frustrated efforts to build a tower to the heavens resulted in the confusion of the nation's languages (11:6-8). But God's relentless search to bring the human family together in oneness continued.

The note sounded throughout the New Testament is grace. Jesus Christ is the embodiment of divine grace. The Gospels unanimously affirm that through Jesus' life, teachings, death, and resurrection, God is working to free humanity from the grip of sin.

Paul's affirmation in Romans 5:8 captures the essence of divine grace: "But God proves his love for us in that while we still were sinners Christ died for us."

The Letter to the Romans, which played a crucial role in Martin Luther's and John Wesley's understanding and experience of salvation, contains Paul's affirmation of the power of grace made known in Jesus Christ (Romans 5; 6).

Ephesians 2:4-8 offers a summary of the New Testament's proclamation of salvation through grace: "God, who is rich in mercy, out of the great love with which he loved us, even when we were dead through our trespasses, made us alive together with Christ. . . . For by grace you have been saved through faith, and this is not your own doing; it is the gift of God." This is the text of Wesley's formative sermon, "The Scripture Way of Salvation."

The most widely used texts in John Wesley's preaching provide a biblical foundation for his distinctive emphasis on salvation by grace. Mark 1:15 appears to have been his favorite New Testament text: "The time is fulfilled, and the kingdom of God has come near; repent, and believe in the good news." In response to God's action in bringing a new world of God's reign, repentance (turning toward the new world) and accepting the good news are the only appropriate responses.

Wesley's favorite text in the Old Testament was Isaiah 55:6-7:
"Seek the LORD while he may be found,
    call upon him while he is near;
let the wicked forsake their way,
    and the unrighteous their thoughts;
let them return to the LORD, that he may
    have mercy on them,
and to our God, for he will abundantly
    pardon."

The entire Bible bears witness to God's grace, from the Creation stories in Genesis to the redemptive acts in the life, death, and resurrection of Jesus the Christ to the promise of a new heaven and a new earth in Revelation. Through the biblical story, God prepares us for salvation (prevenient grace), assures us of forgiveness and claims us as children of God (justifying grace), and nurtures us toward perfect love and holiness (sanctifying grace).

BEHIND WHAT THE *DISCIPLINE* SAYS

Anxious to Prove Ourselves

A high school places exceptional emphasis on competitive scores on standardized academic achievement tests. The prevalent status symbols among the youth of that community are high grade-point averages, enrollment in advanced science courses, and admission to prestigious colleges and universities. Two surveys revealed a startling phenomenon. One indicated that high school students in that community ranked in the upper twenty-fifth percentile on SAT scores; however, in a psychological measurement of self-esteem, those same students rated in the lower twenty-fifth percentile. High academic achievement was not accompanied by an increased sense of self-worth.

Few people in the modern world seem to be worried about religious obedience. Obeying ritualistic laws and fulfilling pious duties occupy little room in the contemporary conscience.

Earning God's favor, even escaping divine punishment, has little hold over most persons today, including many of those people who lead our churches.

Yet the pursuit of a sense of self-worth and personal and social well-being remains a powerful motivator. Efforts to earn salvation (wholeness, health, worth) have merely shifted from the religious to the secular realm. In the modern world, success, prestige, achievement, wealth, knowledge, productivity, athletic prowess and sexual attractiveness have for many people replaced religious rituals and holy duties as means to salvation. Persons feel accepted and whole on the basis of what they *have*, what they *do*, what they *know*, what they *achieve*.

The vocabulary of our cultural mindset replaces *sin* with *failure* and *guilt* with *shame*. Pop psychology becomes a theology. Self-help books become "Scriptures." The latest therapies become "sacraments."

Religious and secular efforts to prove our worth have similar results—emotional stress, judgmentalism, excessive competitiveness, guilt, and failure. Secular legalists use non-religious language for the symptoms of salvation by works, but the psychological and relational dynamics are the same as with those who seek salvation through religious obedience.

Every pastor can provide numerous illustrations of persons who have attempted to earn their identity and worth through accumulating wealth, gaining recognition, earning academic degrees, moving up the success ladder, or some other socially acceptable "good work." Pastors themselves are not immune to this secular form of works righteousness. The size of the church, amount of the salary, position in the denominational hierarchy, and name recognition easily become outward and visible signs of the inner longing for personal worth.

Sin Is for Real

Whether it manifests itself in destructive behavior and values or in misplaced self-worth, sin is real. Various explanations of the nature of sin have been offered by theologians. Reinhold Niebuhr's account of sin as *pride* is well known. Sin is giving in to the inevitable temptation to compete with God for supremacy and control. Sin is thinking too much of ourselves.

On the other hand, sin is also *sloth*, which makes us less than we can be. It is the failure to *be* the sons and daughters of God that we were created to be. Being controlled primarily by our biological and social drives rather than claiming our kinship with the One in whose image we are made—that is sin.

Sin, according to the biblical witness and historical theology, is missing the mark God intends for us. It is failing to actualize our true identity as sons and daughters of God and as loving participants in creation.

Sin is an addition to idols. It is making ultimate that which is finite and temporary and seeking wholeness and fulfillment in anything less than God's grace and purposes. Sin is trying to secure life through such idols as achievement, success, satisfying of appetites. Sin is feeling worthwhile only if others notice us, applaud us, satisfy us. It is participation in structures, habits, and behaviors that resist God's reign of justice, generosity, and joy.

The only one who can save us from sin is the One who is sovereign of all creation, the One in whom "we live and move and have our being" (Acts 17:28). Only God can create and sustain us, love us supremely and permanently, and enable us to be who we really are. We are dependent on God's grace, or else our efforts to gain release from sin only intensify our bondage to it.

WHAT THE *DISCIPLINE* SAYS
(*Discipline*, ¶ 101; student book, pages 7–17)

Wesley's Pilgrimage Toward Grace

John Wesley's pilgrimage of grace began early and continued throughout his life. A home in which disciplined piety, the pursuit of knowledge, religious devotion, and high expectations permeated the atmosphere prepared him for a journey from an identity rooted in works to one rooted in grace. Efforts to attain inner peace through academic pursuits at Oxford, through social service activities in the slums and prisons of London, through cultivating holy habits in the Holy Club at the university, and through missionary service in Georgia were part of his pilgrimage of grace.

Wesley's pilgrimage included a journey from legalism to grace, from an emphasis on justification as a consequence of sanctification to sanctification as a consequence of justification, from faithfulness as an effort to merit grace to faithfulness as an outgrowth of grace.

Wesley's principal concern was "the order of salvation." Albert Outler writes, "The controlling theological inquiry throughout his life was into the meaning of becoming and being a Christian in all the aspects of Christian existence."[1] Obedience, discipline, knowledge, participating in the ordinances of the church, and missional service were always important to Wesley. They seemed to evolve, however, from being means of earning God's favor to being expressions of having received divine grace.

Wesley's Concept of Grace

The key term in Wesleyan theology is *grace*, which the theological statement defines as "the undeserved, unmerited, and loving action of God in human existence through the ever-present Holy Spirit" (*Discipline*, ¶ 101; student book page 12).

Wesley defined *grace* as God's "bounty, or favour: his free, undeserved favour, . . . man having no claim to the least of his mercies. It was free grace that 'formed man of the dust of the ground, and breathed into him a living soul,' and stamped on that soul the image of God, and 'put all things under his feet.' . . . For there is nothing we are, or have, or do, which can deserve the least thing at God's hand."[2]

In his sermon "The Scripture Way of Salvation," Wesley summarized his concept of grace. The sermon, published in 1765, contains part of three earlier sermons—"Salvation by Faith," "Justification by Faith," and "The Circumcision of the Heart." The sermon contains a description of the threefold nature of grace.

Prevenient Grace

One dynamic of grace is *prevenience*. Prevenient grace includes, according to Wesley, "all that is wrought in the soul by what is frequently termed 'natural conscience,' . . . all the 'drawings' of 'the Father,' the desires after God, . . . all that 'light' wherewith the Son of God 'enlighteneth everyone that cometh into the world,' *showing* every man 'to do justly, to love mercy, and to walk humbly with his God'; all the *convictions* which his Spirit from time to time works in every child of man."[3]

Prevenient grace, God's unmerited favor, is present in all creation—in the natural order, in the human conscience, in the relationships and heritage into which we are born. Love of family, the Christian community, the sacraments, creation itself, even pangs of guilt, are vehicles of God's prevenient grace.

Paul Tournier, a contemporary Swiss psychotherapist, accurately described what Wesley understood by prevenient grace: "There comes a day when a man understands that all is of grace, that the whole world is a gift of God, a completely generous gift. . . . We see each flower, each drop of water, each minute of our life as a gift of God."[4]

Wesley described prevenient grace as the porch on a house. It is a place where we prepare to enter the house. Or, grace may be compared to a journey. The desire to make the trip, the road to be traveled, the vehicle in which the journey is to take place, and the map to be followed are all givens. The beauty of the landscape, the mind and the eyes that conceived the journey and perceived its beauty, even the explorer who blazed the trail, are all gifts.

Justifying Grace

Prevenient grace prepares us for *justifying grace*. "Justification," says Wesley, "is another word for pardon. It is the forgiveness of all our sins, and . . . our acceptance with God."[5] *Justifying grace* is the assurance of forgiveness that comes from repentance, from turning toward God's gracious gift of new life. It is being made right with God. It is the acceptance of God's atoning act in Jesus Christ.

Perhaps Wesley's own description of his experience at Aldersgate is the best description of justifying grace: "About a quarter before nine, while he [*the leader*] was describing the change which God works in the heart through faith in Christ, I felt my heart strangely warmed. I felt I did trust in Christ, Christ alone for salvation, and an assurance was given me that he had taken away *my* sins, even *mine*, and saved *me* from the law of sin and death."[6]

For Wesley, justification is conversion. It can be sudden and dramatic or gradual and cumulative. Justifying grace does not remove all doubts or solve our personal problems. It is not a once-for-all experience. Wesley, many years after Aldersgate, raised questions and doubts about his own salvation.

Continuing the analogy of the house, justifying grace is the doorway and the process of walking through it. The door is open with a *Welcome* sign on it. Or if grace is compared to a journey, there comes a time when the traveler packs the bags, joins the guide, and sets out toward the destination. That is justifying grace, the turning toward a new future.

A twenty-seven-year-old inmate in a local jail said to the local United Methodist pastor visiting the jail, "I want God in my life. Tell me how to get God in my life." The pastor asked, "Why is it important for you to have God in your life?" The young man responded by telling the pastor of his guilt, his desire to turn his life around, and his wish to make amends to those persons he had injured.

"You don't have to ask God into your life," said the pastor. "God is already there in your longing for forgiveness, in your desire to make your life count for good, in your wish to repay those you have wronged." (This is prevenient grace.) "Now," added the pastor, "you need but accept God's forgiveness, claim your identity as God's beloved child" (this is justifying grace) "and open all of life to God's presence, and live fully toward the future God wants for you." (This is sanctifying grace.)

Justifying grace is the acceptance of our identity as sons and daughters of God. A five-year-old girl enjoyed her birthday celebration at kindergarten. As her mother picked her up at school, the teacher said, "You know, Ann is a special girl." Ann smiled shyly but appreciatively. As they drove home, the mother said, "Ann, you really are special." Ann replied, "I know. I heard the preacher at church tell me that. He said we are all God's children." That is justifying grace.

One of my most valued possessions is a leather change purse. The thread that holds it together has rotted. The finish is cracked and worn. The fastener barely holds the purse together. The change purse carries no money. It has no utilitarian value. Its value for me lies in knowing to whom it belonged. My grandfather carried the purse in his overalls, and from it he would give coins to his grandson. The purse's worth is rooted in whom it belonged.

Realization of our worth as being rooted in whom we belong is the essence of justifying grace. To accept that identity is to enter the doorway into a whole new existence. It is an identity that we can never earn, nor can it be taken from us.

Sanctifying Grace

Wesley's understanding of grace moves beyond assurance of forgiveness and acceptance of identity as children of God. Without sanctification, grace likely would degenerate into pious narcissism or become "cheap grace," which Dietrich Bonhoeffer identified as forgiveness without repentance and grace without demand.

Sanctifying grace is growth toward perfection. For Wesley, salvation is the total restoration of the divine image in the human personality. As prevenient and justifying grace are thresholds for the Christian life, sanctification is the fulfillment of the divinely given potential to reflect the image of God.

In a sermon entitled "Christian Perfection," Wesley declared that Christian perfection does not imply that Christians are exempt from ignorance, making mistakes, infirmities, or being tempted. He said it is another term for holiness. Sanctification, then, is the continuing process of being made perfect in love and of removing the desire to sin.

Wesley affirmed that God's grace seeks nothing less than a new creation in the likeness of Jesus Christ. As the kingdom of God is both a present reality and a future expectation, personal salvation has both the dimensions of "already" and "not yet."

If prevenient grace is the porch of the house and justification is the doorway, sanctification is the fullness of the house's many rooms. Or, sanctifying grace is continuing a journey with endless possibilities for exploration and ever-expanding horizons.

Each United Methodist minister is asked as a part of his or her ordination and reception into the annual conference, "Are you going on to perfection?" and "Do you expect to be made perfect in love in this life?" One ministerial candidate resisted answering these questions when Bishop Nolan B. Harmon asked them. The bishop asked the hesitant candidate, "If you aren't going on to perfection then what *are* you going toward?"

Conclusion

The distinctive Wesleyan emphasis upon salvation by grace needs to be recovered and proclaimed by United Methodists. Such an emphasis speaks powerfully to a generation seeking an identity rooted not in precarious externals such as achievements and success but in a gift from God.

The emphasis upon prevenient, justifying, and sanctifying grace provides motivation for the pursuit of moral and ethical excellence. Holy living becomes the *fruit* of grace rather than a dogged effort to earn God's favor. Obedience becomes a joy, not a drudgery. Furthermore, since grace is the source of identity and worth, all people are treated with respect and dignity as children of God. We cannot accept Jesus Christ as Savior for us and reject any for whom he died. Grace known in Jesus Christ becomes the primary source of community, not racial or national or ethnic characteristics, or social and economic status.

Hoeing corn was a despised job on the farm. My grandfather each day assigned the number of rows to be hoed before we could quit for the day. One day I began thinking about all my grandfather meant to me. I realized how much he loved me and I him. I decided to hoe more than he required as an expression of love and gratitude. Hoeing corn was never less a burden than when I did it as an expression of gratitude.

The Ten Commandments are prefaced with this assurance of grace: "I am the LORD your God, who brought you ought of the land of Egypt" (Exodus 20:2). The commandments follow as ways of responding to God's redemptive, liberating action. The Christian life is a continuous process of responding to God's prevenient, justifying, and sanctifying grace.

John Wesley affirmed that " 'the doctrine of Christian perfection' was one that 'God [had] peculiarly entrusted to the Methodists,' and had called them out as a separate movement in order 'to spread scriptural holiness over the land.' "[7] Recovery of such an emphasis on holy living as an outgrowth of grace would contribute significantly to a generation seeking moral and ethical direction.

THE SESSION PLAN

1. Have copies of current issues of magazines and newspapers on display on tables in your meeting room. Have this question printed on chalkboard or posterboard: What has gone wrong with the world?

Encourage group members to cut or tear out news material that illustrates something wrong in the world. After a few minutes, invite each participant to comment briefly on one or two items that caught his or her eye. Point out that some stories illustrate the consequences of *personal* actions while others illustrate the consequences of *corporate* actions.

2. According to the Bible, from the very dawn of history human beings have missed the mark of God's intention. We are sinners. Divide the class into four teams. Ask each team to read one of the four stories in Genesis that describe the origin and consequences of sin: Adam and Eve (Genesis 3), Cain and Abel (4:1-24), the Flood (6—9), the tower of Babel (11:1-9). Direct each team to discuss this question: What is sin according to this story?

After allowing about ten minutes for discussion within the teams, have a member of each team report the basic discussion points to the entire class. Then ask the question: How do these stories relate to the problems identified in Activity 1?

Present the material on sin under "Sin Is for Real" on page 44 of this leader's guide.

3. Discuss the material under "Anxious to Prove Ourselves" on pages 43–44 of this leader's guide. Give illustrations of our own addiction to sin, such as the achievement-compulsive lifestyle; our desire to earn worth through recognition, status, wealth, power; our attempts to secure life through control and manipulation. You may ask the class to compare efforts to succeed, win, consume, and accumulate with efforts to earn salvation through religious obedience.

4. Call attention to the entry in the glossary in the student book under *prevenient grace*. Then present the information in the commentary on page 45 of this leader's guide.

5. Ask a member of the class selected in advance to give a brief summary of Wesley's sermon "Justification by Faith." Allow class members to add their comments.

OR

5. To introduce the idea of justifying grace, read aloud the following passage by Frederick Buechner:

> In printers' language to "justify" means to set type in such a way that all full lines are of equal length and flush both left and right; in other words to put the printed lines in the right relationship with the page they're printed on and with each other. The religious sense of the word is very close to this. Being justified means being brought into right relation. Paul says simply that being justified means having peace with God (Romans 5:1). He uses the noun "Justification" for the first step in the process of salvation.
>
> During his Pharisee phase or "blue period," Paul was on his way to Damascus to mop up some Christians when suddenly he heard the voice of Jesus Christ, whose resurrection he had up till now considered only an ugly rumor. What he might have expected the voice to say was "Just you wait." What in effect it did say was "I want you on my side." Paul never got over it.
>
> As far as Paul was concerned, he was the last man in the world for God to have called this way, but God had, thereby revealing himself to be a God who was willing to do business with you even if you were in the process of mopping up Christians at the time. Paul also discovered that all the Brownie points he had been trying to rack up as a super-Pharisee had been pointless. God did business with you not because of who you were but because of who he was.
>
> All the Voice seemed to want Paul to do was believe that it meant what it said and do as it asked. Paul did both.
>
> At a moment in his life when he had least reason to expect it, Paul was staggered by the idea that no matter who you are or what you've done, God wants you on his side. There is nothing you have to do or be. It's on the house. It goes with the territory. God has "justified you," lined you up. To feel this somehow in your bones is the first step on the way to being saved.[8]

Take a minute to invite reactions from group members. Did they find Beuchner's analogy of justification helpful? What other ideas did they have? What other comparisons can they think of to help persons understand justification?

After a brief discussion, read aloud or paraphrase the material on justifying grace on pages 45–46 of this leader's guide.

6. Take a minute to ask group members how they feel about the Wesleyan notion of *sanctification* or *going on to perfection*. Many people think such a goal is presumptuous, even preposterous. To open the issue up in a fresh way, read aloud the paragraph on page 47 of this leader's guide about the question Bishop Nolan B. Harmon asked a ministerial candidate. Then ask these questions: How does the bishop's question put a new twist on the notion of sanctification? Does that new idea help you regard sanctification as a plausible goal?

As a visual aid for thinking about sanctification, draw an *asymptote* on chalkboard or posterboard. *Asymptote* is a mathematical term for a line that gets close and closer to a curve—to infinity—but never quite touches the curve.

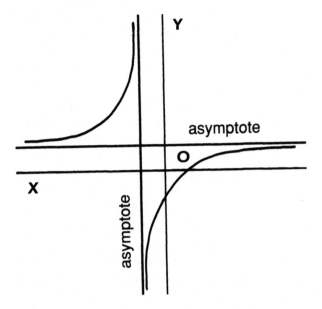

Explain that Wesleyan perfection means perfec*ting*. There always will be new horizons of the love of God and love of neighbor opening up ahead of us. We never get to the point where spiritual progress is no longer possible and desirable. The real issue is not whether we've "arrived," spiritually speaking, but in what direction we're going.

Finally, read aloud or paraphrase the discussion on sanctifying grace on pages 46–47 of this leader's guide.

OR

6. Introduce this step by explaining that sanctifying grace is a matter of ongoing growth so that our minds conform more and more to the mind of Christ. We cannot force that growth to happen, but we can choose to allow God's power to shape us. We can choose to be open or closed to the influence of Christ, day in and day out. And that choice makes a crucial difference. The great American philosopher and psychologist William James is reported to have said, "In a contest between the *will* and the *imagination*, the imagination always wins." If that is so, then the images that we allow to fill our minds become extremely important.

As a way of opening up discussion about sanctifying grace, read aloud the following retelling of Nathaniel Hawthorne's story "The Great Stone Face":

In a spacious valley of many people there lived a boy, the chief character of our story, named Ernest. Like other citizens of his valley he often gazed at a curious formation on the side of a mountain miles away that resembled the face of a man. This Great Stone Face, as it was called, played a large role in the life of the valley. Myths had gathered about the face, myths which prophesied that in the lifetime of those now living a man would appear in the valley who would be the image of the Great Stone Face.

It was a happy lot for children to grow to manhood or womanhood with the Great Stone Face before their eyes, for all the features were noble, and the expression was at once grand and gentle as if it reflected a heart that embraced in its affections all humankind and had room for more.

From his earliest childhood, Ernest longed for the prophecy to come true. Several times in his life he believed briefly that his heart's desire had come to pass. On one occasion the rumor went through the valley that a former resident who had made a great fortune was returning. His name was Gathergold and he was said to resemble the Face. But it was not to be. Gathergold built himself a huge mansion and hoarded his wealth. Soon the people forgot that they had imagined him to be the prophesied man.

Ernest kept his daily communion with the Great Stone Face, always raising the question, "When will you come to our valley?" The face always seemed to reply, "In time I will come."

Later another son of the valley, a soldier who through his valor had been nicknamed Old Blood-and-Thunder, returned to his home. The people hailed him as the fulfiller of the prophecy. "The general! the general!" was now the cry. But Ernest, looking intently into his countenance, sighed, "This is not the man of prophecy." He looked again at the Face of Stone for confirmation.

The next candidate to appear was one who had become an eminent statesman with an eloquence so golden that none could refuse to believe what he said. The citizens of the valley were so sure that he was the prophetic person that they nicknamed him Old Stony Phiz. But again it was not to be. . . .

Years passed and Ernest's hair was turning white. Meanwhile his good sense and quiet wisdom had built for him a reputation that ranged well beyond the valley. People of affairs came from far and near to share the wisdom of this unpretentious man.

One of these visitors was a celebrated poet who had written an eloquent ode to the Great Stone Face. As they came to know one another, the poet and Ernest discovered a deep sharing of sympathies. Listening to the poet, Ernest imagined that the Face was bending forward to listen. He began to hope that here before him was the expected fulfiller of the prophecy. But the poet, realizing Ernest's thoughts, disclaimed the role. He said, "My poetry contains the far-off echo of a heavenly song, but my life, dear Ernest, has not matched my thought." The poet was sad as he spoke and there were tears in his eyes.

Later that evening as Ernest was speaking informally with the visitors who gathered around his cottage, the poet suddenly realized that Ernest's thoughts had reality and depth because they harmonized with the life which he had lived. At last he called out to the listening crowd. "Behold! Behold! Ernest himself is the likeness of the Great Stone Face."

The prophecy was at last fulfilled. The boy who had grown to manhood looking admiringly at the Face had finally grown into his likeness.[9]

Invite group members to discuss the following questions: What sort of character and actions would follow from focusing on Jesus Christ? What persons do you know whose long attention to Christ has molded them according to the mind of Christ? How can *you* focus more intently and consistently on Christ? Are there some things in your life that you need to *stop* focusing on because they are interfering with your devotion to Christ?

Finally, read aloud or paraphrase the discussion of sanctifying grace on pages 46–47 of this leader's guide.

7. Close with singing or reciting the hymn "Amazing Grace" (Number 378 in *The United Methodist Hymnal*).

---

[1] From *The Works of John Wesley, Volume 1,* edited by Albert C. Outler (Abingdon Press, 1984), page 13.

[2] From *The Works of John Wesley, Volume 1,* pages 117–18.

[3] From *The Works of John Wesley, Volume 2,* edited by Albert C. Outler (Abingdon Press, 1985), pages 156–57.

[4] From *The Meaning of Gifts,* by Paul Tournier (John Knox Press, 1963), page 59.

[5] From *The Works of John Wesley, Volume 2,* page 157.

[6] From *The Works of John Wesley, Volume 18,* edited by W. Reginald Ward and Richard P. Heitzenrater (Abingdon Press, 1988), pages 249–50.

[7] From *The Works of John Wesley, Volume 1,* page 85.

[8] Excerpt from *Wishful Thinking: A Theological ABC,* by Frederick Buechner. Copyright © 1973 by Frederick Buechner. Reprinted by permission of Harper & Row, Publishers, Inc.

[9] Reprinted from *New Disciples,* Winter 1986–87, page 28. Copyright © 1986 by Graded Press.

A SENSE OF BALANCE

Purpose of This Session:

To help adults see the genius of United Methodism's sense of balance between faith and good works, between personal assurance and social witness, between knowledge and piety, and between nurture and mission.

Goals of This Session:

1. To promote a better understanding of the relationship between faith and good works, between personal assurance and social witness, between knowledge and piety, and between nurture and mission.
2. To familiarize participants with basic biblical foundations for maintaining this balance.
3. To create and strengthen appreciation for connectional polity as an expression of theological balance.

GROUNDING IN SCRIPTURE

The Old Testament prophets, especially Amos, Hosea, Micah, Isaiah, and Jeremiah, warned their nations against severing faith from practice, personal piety from social responsibility. Amos 5:21-24 is a strong warning against religious practices and perceptions that avoid the requirements of justice:

"I hate, I despise your festivals,
    and I take no delight in your solemn
        assemblies. . . .
Take away from me the noise of your songs;
    I will not listen to the melody of your
        harps.
But let justice roll down like waters,
    and righteousness like an everflowing
        stream."

Such passages throughout the prophetic writings call for a balance between rituals and justice, piety and compassion, personal faith and community responsibility.

Matthew 23 contains a series of indictments of or challenges to some Pharisees. Jesus condemned some Pharisees, for example, for failing to maintain balance between ritualistic practices and justice, mercy, and faith. Apparently, some persons focused on the minute requirements of the tithe while neglecting justice and compassion. They gave too much weight to the social forms of piety and not enough weight to integrity of motives and actions.

Christians need to discard any smugness we may feel when we read Matthew 23. Remember that many of the Pharisees were the moral and religious exemplars of their society, much like the pillars of our Christian churches today. The hypocrisy of *some* Pharisees, which Jesus challenged, is a sin found in *all* religious groups—including Christians. *We* can lose our balance, too!

Salvation by grace through faith, on one hand, and good works, on the other, are parts of the same reality, as Paul's letters clearly demonstrate. In Galatians 3–5, Paul affirms that we are saved by grace and set free from the law. Through the Spirit, we are free from bondage of sin. Yet Paul warns, "You were called to freedom, brothers and sisters; only do not use your freedom as an opportunity for self-indulgence, but through love become slaves to one another" (Galatians 5:13).

The Letter of James may have been written as a counter to those who assumed that faith made works unnecessary. Its message is summarized in 2:14-26. "What good is it . . . if you say you have faith but do not have works? Can faith save you? . . . So faith by itself, if it has no works, is dead" (James 2:14, 17).

The relationship between personal assurance and social witness is affirmed implicitly and explicitly throughout the Bible. Individualism, as we know it, was practically nonexistent in the world of the Bible. The community was of prime importance, but the individual played a key role in the community.

Abraham was called by God to leave his homeland and go toward a new land. God called *Abraham* as an individual. Yet God's call to Abraham included a promise: "I will make of you a great nation, . . . and in you all the families of the earth shall be blessed" (Genesis 12:2-3).

So it is with God's people throughout the biblical story. Individuals experience the reality and presence of God, and that experience brings assurance. God does not reveal the divine purpose or presence for the private, personal enjoyment and benefit of the individual. Rather, the blessing is always intended for the larger community.

In the Gospels, Jesus' ministry includes response to individuals in the midst of their personal needs, yet those same individuals' responses had community ramifications (*see*, for example, Mark 5:1-20).

The Great Commandment (Matthew 22:34-40; Mark 12:28-34; Luke 10:25-28) clearly joins personal assurance with social witness. "You shall love the Lord your God with all your heart, and with all your soul, and with all your strength, and with all your mind; and your neighbor as yourself" (Luke 10:27). Luke follows the giving of the Great Commandment with the story of the good Samaritan (10:29-37), a clear reminder that our relationship with God has implications for our behavior toward others.

The notion that human beings can be separated into mind, body, and soul is also foreign to the Bible. The Hebrews made no separation between loving God with the mind and loving God with the emotions. In other words, the Bible affirms the necessity of responding to God through both knowledge and piety.

In the Old Testament, knowledge is more than a storehouse of facts and information. Knowledge is related to intimate relationships. To know is to experience in the depth of intimacy. In fact, the word *know* is often used for sexual relationships. God's knowledge of the human condition grows out of God's relationship with the human family. God said to Moses, "I have observed the misery of my people who are in Egypt; I have heard their cry on account of their taskmasters. Indeed, I *know* their sufferings, and I have come down to deliver them" (Exodus 3:7-8, italics added).

Knowledge and piety belong together. In Matthew 11:25-28, Jesus established the link between piety, relationship with God, and knowing. True knowledge requires a relationship of obedience and trust in the One who is the source of truth.

In John 8:31-32, Jesus said, "If you continue in my word, you are truly my disciples; and you will know the truth, and the truth will make you free." Again truth is linked with discipleship and genuine piety.

The Bible identifies the church as *both* a nurturing community and a people in mission. The people of Israel were called to be a means of blessing to fellow Israelites as well as the means by which all nations were to be blessed (Genesis 12:3; Isaiah 42:6-7; 49:6). The prophets warned that God's call to the Hebrews was a call to responsibility for others, not a summons to enjoy special privileges.

Paul used the image of the *body* to describe the church (Romans 12:4-8; 1 Corinthians 12). As the body of Christ, the church bears responsibility to nurture its own people, as the various organs of the body support one another. But the church is also to be a transforming agent in the world, a means by which God transforms the world (Romans 12:1-2). The body of Christ consists of diverse gifts that mutually nurture the whole. Yet the principal gift is love, which by its very nature goes beyond the bounds of the church itself (1 Corinthians 13; Ephesians 4:1-16).

The images of the church in 1 Peter 2:4-10 contain both the nurturing and missional dimensions of the church's identity: *royal priesthood, holy nation, God's own people*. The purpose is stated clearly: "in order that you may proclaim the mighty acts of him who called you out of darkness into his marvelous light" (2:9).

The Bible itself, then, affirms theological balance. It clearly undergirds United Methodism's attempt to maintain proper balance between faith and works, between personal assurance and social witness, between knowledge and piety, between the church as a nurturing community and the church as a people in mission.

WHAT THE *DISCIPLINE* SAYS
(*Discipline,* ¶¶ 101, 103, 131; student book, pages 11–14, 31, 40, 58–59)

Heresy, a perversion or distortion of Christian belief, usually results from an overemphasis on one aspect of doctrine at the expense of others. In other words, the failure to maintain appropriate balance leads to heresy. For example, an emphasis on the divinity of Jesus that destroys his humanity distorts the Christian understanding of Jesus' nature and purpose. Or, God's sovereignty can be so emphasized that human freedom is denied.

As a practical theologian, Wesley struck a balance in matters of doctrine and belief. He was not tied to one school of thought but rather adopted the insight of several schools. He subjected all beliefs to the criteria of Scripture, tradition, reason, and experience. The result for Wesley and his heirs has been the maintaining of theological and doctrinal balance.

The emphasis on practical divinity and balance partly accounts for the fact that United Methodists are not identified with one theological or doctrinal affirmation. It is not that United Methodists are indifferent to matters of belief and doctrine. Rather, a distinctive Wesleyan emphasis is that maintaining creative tension and balance is the appropriate response to God's truth, which surpasses all doctrinal formulations.

Faith and Good Works

United Methodists insist that separating faith and good works perverts Christian truth and experience. Faith without works or works without faith—either is heresy. Both are necessary pieces of the fabric of salvation.

Grace, the unmerited favor of God, leads to good works; and efforts to do good works drive us to grace. Some persons are led to grace by first attempting to earn God's favor. The apostle Paul, Martin Luther, and John Wesley are open to receive God's justifying and sanctifying grace only after years of struggle to merit or earn salvation. The early disciples responded to the command "Follow me" only to discover that the One who called them also empowered them to follow him. In other words, their acceptance of Jesus as Lord prepared them to accept him as Savior. Obedience (good works) can be a form of prevenient grace that motivates one to cry out, "God, be merciful to me, a sinner!" (Luke 18:13).

While some people may begin their pilgrimage toward wholeness with attempting to be obedient, others may begin the journey with an experience of forgiveness and acceptance that motivates good works. The woman caught in the act of adultery, for example, heard first an assurance of forgiveness, "Where are they [*your accusers*]? Has no one condemned you? . . . Neither do I condemn you." Then followed the command, "Go your way, and from now on do not sin again" (John 8:10-11).

Wesley parted with the Moravians partly over the matter of faith and good works. The Moravians, along with others, believed that good works without the assurance of having been justified were but "splended sins." Wesley strongly challenged such a claim. He followed the advice of Peter Böhler, who told him, "Preach faith *till* you have it, and then, *because* you have it, you *will* preach faith."[1] Wesley also differed from the Calvinists on the matter of good works. The Calvinists denied any validity to *natural* virtue. Wesley, however, considered virtue and the human conscience as expressions of grace, prevenient grace.

United Methodists affirm that both faith and good works are manifestations of grace. Wesley considered that God makes no demands without providing the grace to meet the demands. So both the commands and the power to fulfill them are rooted in God's grace.

For United Methodists, the Christian life is an ongoing, dynamic pilgrimage of holy living, moving toward being made perfect in love. The journey consists of seeking to follow the commands of God, receiving forgiveness and restoration for failing to follow, and out of gratitude for the forgiveness and restoration, striving all the more to be obedient. Discipleship, then, means keeping alive the tension and balance between faith and good works.

Personal Assurance and Social Witness

Maintaining a proper balance between personal salvation and social witness is a hallmark of the Wesleyan heritage. When one is emphasized at the expense of the other, doctrinal heresy and distorted piety are the results.

Personal salvation without witness to and involvement in the transformation of society reduces God to a domesticated deity whose principal concern is personal happiness. Religion becomes the supreme appeal to selfishness and narcissism. The ultimate test of religion's truth and validity becomes its ability to resolve a person's inner conflicts and enable him or her to accomplish personal goals.

Social witness and transformation without personal assurance becomes mere "do-good-ism," and it generally results in disillusionment or violence or both. The assurance of the reconciling grace of God keeps social action alive and redemptive. Assurance of God's love transforms individuals and social structures. Those who know and accept their identity as sons and daughters of the living God become as leaven and the salt. They know that all does not depend upon them but that through the faithfulness of God's people, God's power transforms the world.

Methodism has a long history of uniting personal assurance and social witness in both theory and practice. As the *Discipline* states, "For Wesley there is no religion but social religion, no holiness but social holiness" (¶ 101; student book, page 14).

John Wesley was clear on the unity of personal religion and social witness. He said that Christianity is essentially a social religion and that turning it into a solitary religion can destroy it. Personal salvation is known and shared in a community of faith. Personal salvation expresses itself in efforts to reform society into a realm in which God reigns supreme.

John Wesley was deeply and personally involved with the poor, the prisoners, and the outcasts of eighteenth-century England. He spoke out courageously and prophetically on issues such as slavery, economic exploitation, the abuse of alcohol, and all kinds of corruption. His involvement in the Sunday school movement, in ministry with the poor, in prison reform, and in efforts to abolish slavery is evidence of his attempts to respond programmatically to society's needs.

The commitment to social transformation is clear from Wesley's own inclusion of the following in the minutes of the conferences dating back to 1763: "What may we reasonably believe to be God's design in raising up the preachers called Methodists? Not to form any new sect, but to reform the nation, particularly the Church, and to spread spiritual holiness over the land."[2]

Knowledge and Vital Piety

Most history books identify the eighteenth century as the Age of Reason. Religious writers, focusing on the revivals that warmed hearts in Europe, England, and America, have called it a new age of faith. But it was also a time when people were torn between faith and reason, between theology and science, between classical Christianity and natural religion. Some chose the rationalistic tenets of deism, while others sought the warm inner feelings of heartfelt religion. Knowledge and piety diverged.

The Wesleys, however, refused to participate in the split between reason and faith. They and their United Methodist descendants have sought to maintain a balance between knowledge and piety.

Carved in stone near the entrance to the library building at Wesley Seminary in Washington, D.C., is a quotation from one of Charles Wesley's hymns: "Unite the pair so long disjoined, knowledge and vital piety." The layout of Wesley Seminary symbolizes United Methodism's commitment to both knowledge and piety. The library and chapel are located and designed in such a way that as one sits in the library, the chapel altar is clearly visible, and as one leaves the chapel, one faces the library.

Piety without knowledge becomes superficial emotionalism and easy prey to heresy. On the other hand, knowledge without piety removes the transcendent and elevates the human mind to supremacy. As John Wesley declared in a daring sermon preached at Saint Mary's, Oxford, August 24, 1744, "Without love [for God] all learning is but splendid ignorance."[3]

Methodism's heritage combines in theory and practice a commitment to both the cultivation of personal piety and the pursuit of knowledge. Wesley was a well-rounded scholar with an exceptional intellectual curiosity. He was well schooled in the classics and read them to approach issues from a historical as well as a theological perspective.

Wesley expected scholarship from his preachers and devoted himself to providing intellectual as well as spiritual leadership. He participated in the Sunday school movement started by Robert Raikes. Originally the Sunday school was an effort to educate poor children in the basics of reading, writing, and arithmetic as well as exposing them to the stories of the Bible.

The insistence upon maintaining both vital piety and knowledge enables United Methodists to love God with the mind and the heart. It also promotes a wholistic view of reality that affirms that all truth is from God and must be used to promote the purposes of God for creation. While valuing education and learning, United Methodists contend that knowledge in and of itself is insufficient. Knowledge guided by love for God and love for persons expressed in the pursuit of knowledge represent a distinctive emphasis of "the people called Methodists." It is an emphasis uniquely needed in today's world.

Nurture and Mission

Some critics contend that United Methodism has no clear ecclesiology, or doctrine of the church. However, the Wesleyan tradition lays some firm foundations for a strong and helpful understanding of the church's nature and mission. Local United Methodist churches would do well to examine their own self-understanding in light of the Wesleyan balance between the church as a nurturing fellowship and the church as a community in mission.

Local churches may succumb to the temptation to distort their divinely given nature and purpose by failing to maintain equilibrium between the church as a compassionate community of nurture and the church as the community's prophetic conscience.

An emphasis on nurture without a commitment to global mission reduces the church to an ecclesiastical or spiritual spa that caters to the personal interests of its members. Its fellowship is reduced to superficial smiles and glad handshakes, and its mission is limited to helping nice people be nicer. It becomes a pious club that exists for the well-being of its members instead of being the people of God who exist for the world God seeks to redeem, a sign and herald of God's kingdom.

On the other hand, an emphasis on mission without being a nurturing community reduces the church to a social service agency that ignores the deep spiritual needs of persons and the transcendent dimensions of God's activity. Mission without the nurture of the individual's and congregation's total well-being tends to undermine the church's witness in political action and social service. The foundation and motivation for mission begin to crumble. Wesley's involvement in the social, economic, and political issues and problems of his time was not motivated by a general humanitarianism. Instead, it was part and parcel of his discipleship and evangelical witness to the power of the gospel of Jesus Christ to transform all of creation.

From Wesley's time to the present, Methodism has sought to be both a nurturing community and a servant community. Members of the Methodist societies and class meetings met for personal nurture through study, worship, prayer, and admonition of one another. They also were involved in mission through giving to the poor, visiting the imprisoned, and working for justice and peace in the community. They sought not only to receive the fullness of God's grace for themselves; but as we have seen, they saw themselves as existing "to reform the nation . . . and to spread scriptural holiness over the land" (*Discipline*, ¶ 101; student book, page 11).

Before Methodism became a church, it was a

mission. Therefore, its structure and organization originated as means of accomplishing the mission of spreading "scriptural holiness over the land." From the beginning, The United Methodist Church has been a connectional church. That is, the local church is connected to the larger structure.

Connectional polity has been considered by Wesley's descendants as the most effective and appropriate means of being both a nurturing community and a community in mission. No local church is the total body of Christ and so cannot adequately, by itself, reflect God's redemptive activity on behalf of the whole world. Consequently, United Methodist churches are bound together by a common mission and a common polity. Through the connectional bond, United Methodists join in mission with other denominations as well as with other United Methodist churches and organizations.

The theological statement in the *Discipline* claims our identity as a nurturing fellowship and servant community in mission: "Connectional ties bind us together in faith and service in our global witness, enabling faith to become active in love and intensifying our desire for peace and justice in the world" (¶ 101; student book, page 14).

Conclusion

United Methodism's unique contribution to the broader Christian community does not lie in a specific doctrine. Rather, it lies in an emphasis on maintaining balance in critical matters of Christian belief and practice. Proclamation in word and practice of faith and good works, personal assurance and social witness, knowledge and vital piety, and nurture and mission will enable The United Methodist Church to be a vital community of faith in a fragmented and divided world.

THE SESSION PLAN

1. Briefly review the previous session by stating that United Methodism claims no unique doctrines but rather is known for its particular emphases. One of those emphases, which the group will look at in this session, is *balance* in matters of faith and doctrine.

2. In groups of three to five persons each, discuss heresy as an overemphasis of one dimension of belief at the expense of other dimensions. Ask each group to give illustrations of such imbalance. Examples that may emerge are

- an emphasis on "being saved" that implies that salvation is a once-and-for-all experience with no growth necessary;
- being Christian means obeying the Ten Commandments and living by the Golden Rule;
- being Christian means having the right beliefs with behavior and experience having minimal importance;
- being "right with God" is all that matters;
- personal religious experience that has no consequences in relationships in the broader world;
- social service activities and involvement without a personal relationship with Christ.

Ask the class to compare contemporary examples of imbalance with illustrations from the Bible. (Recall Amos's criticism of Israel and Judah and Jesus' conflicts with the Pharisees and Sadducees.)

3. Have Articles IX and X of the Articles of Religion and Articles IX and X of the Confession of Faith printed on posterboard and posted on a wall. Refer to them and then review the material on "Faith and Good Works" in this leader's guide. Distinguish between accepting Jesus as Lord and accepting Jesus as Savior. Ask these questions: How would you describe your initial experience of Christ—as Lord or as Savior? Looking back over your religious pilgrimage, which has been a stronger emphasis in your life—faith or works, grace, or obedience?

Allow persons an opportunity to report on their journeys, especially their attempts to maintain balance between faith and good works.

4. On posterboard write this statement: "This church should stick to preaching the gospel

and leave social issues alone." Immediately beneath that statement write "Agree" and "Disagree" as the headings for two columns. Then ask group members to suggest reasons people typically give for agreeing or disagreeing with such a statement. Record their suggestions in the appropriate columns.

After a few minutes, read aloud this quotation from John Wesley: "The Gospel of Christ knows no religion but social; no holiness, but social holiness." Then read or paraphrase the material under "Personal Assurance and Social Witness" in this leader's guide.

If time allows, ask class members to list the issues in society that they think The United Methodist Church should address and to suggest ways those issues might be addressed. How can their suggestions incorporate a proper balance of faith and works?

5. Copy ahead of time onto posterboard these lyrics from Charles Wesley's hymn "Come, Father, Son, and Holy Ghost":

Come, Father, Son, and Holy Ghost,
To whom we for our children cry;
The good desired and wanted most
Out of thy richest grace supply;
The sacred discipline be given,
To train and bring them up for heaven.

Error and ignorance remove,
Their blindness both of heart and mind;
Give them the wisdom from above,
Spotless and peaceable and kind;
In knowledge pure their mind renew,
And store with thoughts divinely true.

Unite the pair so long disjoined,
Knowledge and vital piety;
Learning and holiness combined,
And truth and love let all men see
In these, whom up to thee we give,
Thine, wholly thine, to die and live.

Father, accept them in thy Son,
And ever by thy Spirit guide!
Thy wisdom in their lives be shown,
Thy name confessed and glorified;
Thy power and love diffussed abroad,
Till all our earth is filled with God.[4]

Explain to the class that Charles Wesley wrote this hymn for the 1748 opening of Kingswood School for boys, which was founded by John Wesley. The curriculum included reading, writing, mathematics, languages, sciences, history, geography, music, and the Christian religion.

Invite the class to sing the hymn (to the tune of "Faith of Our Fathers") or to read the words aloud together. Then present the material on knowledge and vital piety in the sections "Grounding in Scripture" and "Knowledge and Vital Piety" on pages 51–52 and 54–55 of this leader's guide.

On the basis of that material, discuss the statement that education is the world's greatest need. You might point out that Nazism took root in Germany, the most educated nation in the world during the 1930s and 1940s. Yet some of the world's greatest atrocities have been committed by pious people who seemingly lacked reason and knowledge.

OR

5. To launch discussion of the value of knowledge *and* vital piety, ask what group members think about contemporary novelist Walker Percy's statement in *The Second Coming* that one can "get all A's and still flunk life." What is the difference between wisdom and intellectual brilliance? What impact can vital piety have on character flaws such as arrogance, egoism, and pride that often accompany intellectual superiority? Draw upon the material in "Knowledge and Vital Piety" in this leader's guide as needed.

6. Summarize the material regarding "Nurture and Mission" in this leader's guide. Distribute copies of your local church weekly calendar. Ask group members to mark each event on the calendar with either an *N* (Nurture) or an *M* (Mission). Some may be appropriately labeled as both *N* and *M*. Count the number of *N*s and *M*s. Ask this question: What does this tally say about our church's balance between nurture and mission? You might want to do the same activity with a copy of the church budget.

7. United Methodism is perhaps better known for its connectional polity than for its doctrines. This leader's guide implies that our connectional structure is a reflection of our understanding of the nature and mission of the church. If that is true, what does our connectionalism affirm about the church? Among other things, it affirms that the *local* church is not the total body of Christ. Instead, the local church is one organ of the body.

Review the structure of The United Methodist Church by diagramming it in the form of a body.[5] Copy the sketch on this page[6] (much larger, of course) on a large piece of posterboard. Then cut up the figure into as many pieces as you have class members to make a jigsaw puzzle. Pass out the puzzle pieces, inviting group members to work together to assemble the puzzle. After the puzzle is assembled, you may need to point out that The United Methodist Church extends beyond the borders of the United States.

8. Summarize the session by reading or restating the "Conclusion" section in this leader's guide.

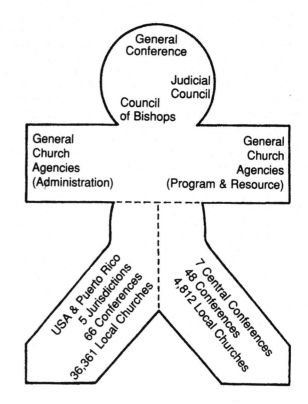

---

[1] From *The Works of John Wesley, Volume 18*, edited by W. Reginald Ward and Richard P. Heitzenrater (Abingdon Press, 1988), page 228.

[2] From *The Works of John Wesley, Volume 1*, edited by Albert C. Outler (Abingdon Press, 1984), page 85.

[3] From *The Works of John Wesley, Volume 1*, page 176.

[4] From *The Book of Hymns*, Copyright © 1968, Board of Publication of The United Methodist Church, Number 344.

[5] For detailed information about the structure of the general church agencies, see the sixty-eight-page booklet, *Organizational Charts of the General Agencies of The United Methodist Church* (General Council on Ministries, 1989).

[6] Art by Bill Woods.

Session 7

DOCTRINE AND DISCIPLINE

Purpose of This Session:
To help adults see the doctrine and discipline belong together in United Methodism and that the General Rules can offer direction today.

Goals of This Session:
1. To help group members identify connections between sound doctrine and disciplined living.
2. To be able to state the General Rules of the United Societies and to discuss their continuing relevance.
3. To motivate persons to live a lifestyle that reflects the gospel.

GROUNDING IN SCRIPTURE

The United Methodist accent on sound doctrine and disciplined, holy living resonates with the biblical emphasis on call and response, grace and command, freedom and responsibility, faith and works. The biblical concept of a covenant community, called into being by God and characterized by faithfulness and mutual support, provides the foundation for the early Methodist Societies and class meetings.

As a covenant people, Israel was bound to God by a call to be God's people. God had freed them from bondage, given them an identity, and molded them into a community. In response to God's steadfast love and faithfulness, they were to live in accordance with God's commandments (Exodus 20:1-17). Since God is holy, they too were to be holy (Leviticus 11:44-45; 19:1-2; 20:7-8). Belief in God's covenant relationship with Israel carried with it the obligation on their part to behave as God's people.

Claiming an identity as the people of God without the accompanying responsibility to act with justice, righteousness, and fidelity to the covenant resulted in God's judgment. That was the warning given by the prophets Amos, Hosea, Micah, Isaiah, Jeremiah, and Ezekiel. The prophets insisted that God's purpose for Israel and presence with Israel meant that Israel had exceptional responsibility, not special privilege. God called them to social justice and to individual and collective righteousness.

The New Testament maintains the balance between belief and practice. Jesus went along the lakeside announcing the good news of God's reign (doctrine) and calling upon people to repent, to turn toward the new world God is bringing (discipline) (Mark 1:14-15). He warned those who would substitute correct beliefs and proper affirmations for *doing* God's will, "Not everyone who says to me, 'Lord, Lord,' will enter the kingdom of heaven, but only the one who does the will of my Father in heaven" (Matthew 7:21). Jesus summoned persons to a life of single-minded, disciplined devotion (Matthew 10:37-39; 16:24-26; Mark 8:34; Luke 9:23; 14:17). The Sermon on the Mount challenged the disciples to unparalleled goodness (Matthew 5–7). It is an unself-conscious goodness that cannot be attained by effort but can emerge only from a relationship with the Christ.

Paul proclaimed with vigor born of experience that God had brought redemption through Jesus Christ. The doctrine of justification by faith was a basic theme of his preaching and teaching (Romans 5:1-11; 2 Corinthians 5:17-19; Galatians 2:16-21; Ephesians 2:8). Yet Paul also preached that the doctrine of salvation through the grace of Jesus Christ called one to live in a "manner worthy of the gospel of Christ" (Philippians 1:27). Christ's sacrificial love, according to Paul, summons us to a life that shuns impurity, covetousness, improper speech, deception, drunkenness, debauchery (Ephesians 5:1-20). He warned the Galatians that they were not to use their freedom "as an opportunity for self-indulgence" (Galatians 5:13). They were to deny "the works of the flesh," which include "fornication, impurity, licentiousness, idolatry, sorcery, enmities, strife, jealousy, anger, quarrels, dissensions, factions, envy, drunkenness, carousing, and things like these" (5:19-21). They were to exhibit the fruit of the Spirit, "love, joy, peace, patience, kindness, generosity, faithfulness, gentleness, and self-control" (5:22-23).

The Letter of James explicitly connects sound doctrine with holy living. The letter may have been written to counter the notion that sound doctrine is sufficient. To those who would limit religion to faith, James counters, "Religion that is pure and undefiled before God, the Father, is this: to care for orphans and widows in their distress, and to keep oneself unstained by the world" (James 1:27). The letter is a call to combine faith and works in a life that fulfills "the royal law . . . 'You shall love your neighbor as yourself'" (2:8).

Scripture supports the three ethical principles of the General Rules; doing no harm and avoiding evil of every kind, doing good of every possible sort, and attending upon all the ordinances of God. The Ten Commandments, for example, call for doing no harm—not killing, committing adultery, stealing, bearing false witness, coveting, or taking the Lord's name in vain. They also call for doing good and giving proper place to the Holy One—letting God be sovereign of life, keeping the sabbath, honoring father and mother (Exodus 20:1-17; Deuteronomy 5:6-21). The Sermon on the Mount (Matthew 5–7) calls for doing no harm—no anger, adultery, lust, false witness, vengeance, or judging others. It also is a summons to be and to do good—mercy, forgiveness of others, trusting in God, discipline. The Sermon on the Mount acknowledges the importance of holy habits—almsgiving, prayer, fasting.

Paul's distinction in Galatians 5:19-23 between the works of the flesh and the fruit of the Spirit sounds amazingly similar to John Wesley's "doing no harm" and "doing good of every possible sort." Further, the specific examples of harm and good in Wesley's Rules and Paul's Letter to the Galatians have much in common.

The General Rules are well grounded in Scripture in form, content, and spirit. The existence of the societies and classes for the purpose of nurture and support in holy living through living in accordance with the General Rules is reminiscent of the covenant communities of Israel and the apostolic church.

WHAT THE *DISCIPLINE* SAYS
(*Discipline*, ¶¶ 101, 103; student book, pages 15–17, 39–42)

As Session 6 demonstrates, United Methodism has a tradition of maintaining balance in doctrinal and theological matters. The balance also is reflected in the emphasis given to both sound doctrine and disciplined living. Doctrine in the Wesleyan tradition serves the purposes of character formation, ethical living, and evangelical proclamation. Sound doctrine serves to shape persons and communities into the image of God. The balanced combination of right thinking and holy living existed in Wesley's own experiences as a child in the Epworth rectory, as a student at Charterhouse in London, as a scholar and teacher at Oxford, and as a diligent priest of the national church.

Wesley's disciplined life was intensified while he was at Oxford. By 1732, Wesley had gathered around him a group of five or six persons who shared his commitment to disciplined Christian living. The group was referred to as the Oxford Methodists and the Holy Club. In addition to devoting themselves to study, prayer, self-examination, and mutual admonition, they visited prisons twice each week, spent an hour or two every week in visiting the sick, and regularly ministered to the poor. They resolved to do good to as many persons as possible and to refrain from all forms of evil.

It should be no surprise, then, that when in 1739 eight or ten persons came to Wesley seeking advice and assistance "to flee from the wrath to come," Wesley arranged to meet with them weekly. This was the rise of the United Societies. The only requirement for admission in the societies was "a desire to flee from the wrath to come, and to be saved from their sins." They met together "in order to pray together, to receive the word of exhortation, and to watch over one another in love, that they may help each other to work out their salvation" (*Discipline*, ¶ 103; student book, page 40).

Further Description of Societies and Classes

The United Societies and classes emerged as a response to the need for nurture in Christian doctrine and living. Eighteenth-century English society was not known for its discipline and morality. It was a time of hedonism and rebellion against traditional norms of morality. Debauchery was epidemic among all classes of citizens. Life was cheap, and exploitation of children and the poor was rampant. Wealth was concentrated in a few members of the nobility. The church had little relationship to the working class, and religion suffered from many conflicting currents—from indifference to fanaticism, from rationalism to emotionalism.

Philosophically, eighteenth-century England was dominated by rationalism and deism. Reason was exalted as the highest gift of God, and God was removed from the realm of human experience. Interest in religion tended to be limited to two extremes—intellectual curiosity and mystic superstition.

Such a social and religious climate made it difficult for persons to maintain either sound doctrine or holy living. It is understandable, then, that those who genuinely wanted to pursue holiness formed groups that fostered such pursuit.

The societies grew rapidly. As they grew, they were divided into *classes,* consisting of about twelve people who lived near one another. One member was designated as the leader. The leader's responsibilities included weekly visits to each class member, keeping the ministers and stewards of the society informed about people who needed particular attention, and delivering aid to the poor. Leaders were expected to keep informed as to the spiritual and moral well-being of class members and offer comfort and exhortation as situations warranted.

Members of the societies and classes were expected to participate in the sacraments and worship of the established church. They did not see themselves as a separatist movement. Their goal was personal and social transformation, not to form an alternative church.

The General Rules represent a concise statement of the ethical and moral principles and practices expected of those who, in response to God's grace, seek to live holy lives. The Rules specified the behavior expected. The classes and societies provided the support, encouragement, and challenge for living the expectations.

Three-Part Formula for Holy Living

Desire for salvation, according to Wesley, must manifest itself, *first,* "By doing no harm, by avoiding evil of every kind" (*Discipline*, ¶103; student book, page 40). The list of harmful behavior includes profaning God's name, abuse of the Lord's day, drunkenness and buying or selling "spirituous liquors," buying or selling or holding slaves, fighting and quarreling, seeking vengeance and retaliation, harmful speaking of others, extravagant display, singing and reading that does not promote the knowledge and love of God, self-indulgence, "laying up treasure upon earth," failing to pay debts.

Wesley's rules cannot be dismissed as merely quaint and obsolete. The first rule, "Do no harm," for instance, seems to foreshadow the interest of contemporary ethicists in the *principle of nonmaleficence.*[1] *Nonmaleficence* is the refraining from harming or injuring others. It rules out any form of harm or injury, including injury to reputation, to property, and to liberty. Nonmaleficence forbids both willful and unintentional harm. Even taking undue risks of harming is prohibited. Driving while intoxicated, for example, is a violation of the principle of nonmaleficence because it involves taking a risk that harm will result. It is possible to violate the duty of nonmaleficence without acting maliciously or even without being aware of or intending the risk of harm, and the violation may involve omission or commission. The principle demands that persons act thoughtfully and carefully, exploring potential consequences of particular behavior.

The principle of nonmaleficence is akin to the Sermon on the Mount in including intention behind the act. One must not only refrain from murder but avoid the anger that risks murder. One must not only resist the act of adultery but also the lust that intends adultery. Nonmaleficence and Wesley's "Do no harm" rule are helpful principles in a world in which individualism, self-interest, and self-indulgence cause in incalculable harm and injury.

Members of the societies were expected to evidence their desire for salvation, *second,* "By doing good; by being in every kind merciful after their power; as they have opportunity, doing good of every possible sort, and, as far as possible, to all" (*Discipline,* ¶ 103; student book, page 41).

Doing good includes providing for physical needs such as food, clothing, medical care, and visiting the sick and imprisoned (as in Matthew 25:31-46). It involves responding to spiritual needs by providing counsel, discipline, and comfort. Doing good includes social responsibility and mutual support of brothers and sisters in the faith. Private acts of helpfulness, though important, are insufficient.

Wesley's second rule seems to have anticipated another idea in contemporary ethical thought: the *principle of beneficence.*[2] Nonmaleficence refers to noninfliction of harm on others. Beneficence requires that we contribute to the health and well-being of others. While nonmaleficence requires that we refrain from doing harm, beneficence requires positive steps to help others.

Beneficence includes efforts to *prevent* harm as well as the *removal* of harmful conditions. For example, simply providing food, clothing, and medical care to the poor may be an expression of beneficence. However, beneficence also includes the duty to remove the social, economic, and political causes of poverty. Wesley was not content to provide aid to prisoners and slaves. He sought to reform the prison system and to abolish slavery. He not only admonished

against drunkenness; he also prohibited profiting from selling intoxicants.

Wesley's principle of doing all the good one can and its contemporary expression in the principle of beneficence challenge United Methodists to broaden their ethical and moral concerns beyond the private sphere to include the social, economic, and political dimensions of life. Prophetic witness and social ministries are required of those who seek "to reform the nation . . . and to spread scriptural holiness over the land." Doing good includes the removal of the conditions that threaten the well-being of the creation God loves and the promotion of the conditions that foster peace, justice, and righteousness.

Members of the societies also had to evidence their desire for salvation, *third,* "By attending upon all the ordinances of God," including public worship, the ministry of the Word, the sacrament of the Lord's Supper, family and private prayer, searching the Scriptures, and fasting or abstinence (*Discipline,* ¶ 103; student book, page 42).

There is a sense in which doing no harm and doing good are outgrowths of "attending upon all the ordinances of God." Public worship, the sacraments, prayer, study of Scripture, and fasting and abstinence keep the channels of grace open. The ordinances of the church perpetually confront us with the truth and presence of God, and it is through the ordinances that God renews and empowers us to refrain from doing harm and to do good.

Wesley's own experience and his Rules for the Societies are reminders that United Methodist interest in faith formation and spiritual discipline are no passing fads or new developments. When the church was formed in America in 1784, Wesley sent *The Sunday Service of the Methodists in North America with Other Services.* Among the "other services" was "The Order for Morning Prayer." Wesley intended that members of the Methodist societies in America would incorporate such services into their daily practice. His willingness to have Francis Asbury ordained and designated superintendent was largely for the sacramental needs of the American Methodists. Asbury proceeded to ordain clergy so that Methodists could right-fully attend upon all the ordinances of God.

Conclusion

In the United Methodist tradition, doctrine and discipline belong together. In a hedonistic, narcissistic age, the traditional United Methodist emphasis on holy living and sound doctrine is sorely needed. And in an era when individualism contributes to personal loneli-ness and social fragmentation, a recovery of covenant communities of mutual support can contribute significantly to the reform of the nation and to the spread of holiness.

The General Rules contain the basic frame-work of sound ethical living. The complexity of some current moral dilemmas requires a rethinking or elaboration of Wesley's specific guidelines; however, the general principles of doing no harm, doing all the good one can, and attending to the ordinances of God as means of faith formation provide a basis for fur-ther discussion and responsible action.

THE SESSION PLAN

1. Begin the session with a brief review of Session 6 by writing the following phrases on chalkboard or posterboard:
• "Faith and Good Works"
• "Personal Assurance and Social Witness"
• "Knowledge and Vital Piety"
• "Nurture and Mission"
Comment on the United Methodist emphasis on maintaining balance in matters of faith. When an emphasis is placed on *one* dimension only of any of the above pairs, the Christian *faith* and *life* are distorted. Tell group members that during this session they will consider another dimension of the religious life where United Methodists strive to maintain proper balance. Add this phrase to the list: "Doctrine and Discipline."

2. In order for class members to see the rela-tionship between affirmation of belief and sub-sequent response in the Bible, scramble the following affirmation-and-response couplets and ask class members to match affirmations with the appropriate responses:

Affirmation: "I am the LORD your God, who brought you out of the land of Egypt" (Exodus 20:2).
Response: "You shall have no other gods before me" (Exodus 20:3).

Affirmation: "Hear, O Israel: The LORD is our God, the LORD alone" (Deuteronomy 6:4).
Response: "You shall love the LORD your God with all your heart, and with all your soul, and with all your might" (Deuteronomy 6:5).

Affirmation: "For I am the LORD your God" (Leviticus 11:44).
Response: "Sanctify yourselves therefore, and be holy, for I am holy" (Leviticus 11:44).

Affirmation: "The time is fulfilled, and the king-dom of God has come near" (Mark 1:15).
Response: "Repent, and believe in the good news" (Mark 1:15).

Affirmation: "In Christ God was reconciling the world to himself" (2 Corinthians 5:19).
Response: "And entrusting the message of recon-ciliation to us" (2 Corinthians 5:19).

Affirmation: "For you were called to freedom" (Galatians 5:13).
Response: "Only do not use your freedom as an opportunity for self-indulgence, but through love be slaves to one another" (Galatians 5:13).

Affirmation: "In this is love, not that we loved God but that he loved us and sent his Son to be the atoning sacrifice for our sins" (1 John 4:10).
Response: "Beloved, since God loved us so much, we also ought to love one another" (1 John 4:11).

Affirmation: "Once you were not a people, but now you are God's people; once you had not received mercy, but now you have received mercy" (1 Peter 2:10).
Response: "Beloved, I urge you as aliens and exiles to abstain from the desires of the flesh that wage war against the soul" (1 Peter 2:11).

Print an affirmation on one card and the accompanying response on another card. (Do not write the Scripture reference on the cards.) Distribute the affirmations to half the class and the responses to the other half. Have class members find their "partner" by matching affirmations and responses. Provide Scripture references to those who are unable to find their matching partner. Additional Scripture passages that can be used are John 8:12; John 10:9; John 15:9; Ephesians 2:10.

3. Clarify that since John Wesley's emphasis was upon "practical divinity," he was concerned about relating doctrine to life. His understanding of sanctification as a continuous process of being made perfect in love, his own experiences as a child and as a member of the Holy Club at Oxford, his earnest desire to live a holy life, and his conviction that God had called the Methodists to "spread scriptural holiness over the land," all helped to lay the foundation for the formation of the United Societies and classes. Briefly describe the societies and classes by using the material on pages 60–61 in this leader's guide.

Ask class members if any of them have been members of comparable groups. Examples might be support groups, ongoing Bible study groups or prayer groups in the home, therapy groups, Alcoholics Anonymous, and the like. How are these groups similar to the societies and classes? How are they different? What "rules" do these groups have?

4. Call attention to the General Rules, printed on student book pages 39–42. Have group members read them silently, marking with a plus sign (+) those they would recommend keeping, a minus sign (-) those they would eliminate, and a question mark (?) those about which they are uncertain.

5. While class members are reading the General Rules, write on chalkboard or posterboard in column form three categories:
• Do no harm (nonmaleficence).
• Do good to all (beneficence)
• Attend ordinances.

Point out to the group that the first two categories are strikingly similar to the ethical principles of nonmaleficence and beneficence as described in this leader's guide.

Divide the group into two teams. Assign one of the following cases, or a case that you have prepared, to each team and ask team members to discuss it in light of the principles of doing no harm (nonmaleficence) and doing good (beneficence).

Case One: A young man, age eighteen, breaks into the church. He breaks stained-glass windows and destroys other property. The alarm system warns the police, who come and arrest the intruder. He is injured in the process of entering the building and is taken to the local hospital. He tests positive for several illegal drugs and has no recollection of breaking into the church. The pastor decides to visit the young man in the hospital and learns that he has a history of drug abuse. His father and mother are divorced, and he lived most of his childhood with his elderly grandparents. His father is rather wealthy but has given up on trying to help his son. The young man says that the experience has convinced him that he needs help, and he agrees to enter a drug treatment program. The district attorney contacts the church and says, "The church must press charges before we can prosecute the case." As members of the congregation, what do you recommend, based upon the General Rules?

Cast Two: The State Department of Correction has proposed to locate a minimum-security prison in the community in which your church is located. Many of the prisoners will be on work release and will be going to work in local factories and business during the day. A meeting is held at the church to discuss the proposal. Some citizens have expressed strong opposition to having the facility in the community. As church members and citizens, you have just studied Wesley's General Rules. On what basis would you come to your position?

6. Return to the copy of the General Rules in the student book. Ask class members to report on their review of the rules. List under the headings specifics they would retain, delete, question. Spend some time discussing what contemporary "rules" they would add.

7. Stephen Mott, in *Biblical Ethics and Social Change,* describes the church as a "counter-community."[3] As a counter-community the church is to affirm and live alternative norms and values to those of the broader society. The Methodist Societies and classes represented a counter-community to the prevailing culture of eighteenth-century England. One way to make the General Rules relevant to the contemporary culture would be to contrast prevailing values and norms in the culture with those of the reign of God. You might do that simply by listing them beside each other. Here are some examples:

Culture	*Counter-Community*
Aggressiveness	Meekness, gentleness
Power as force	Power as love
Winning, being Number 1	Last shall be first
Greatness as being served	Greatness as serving
Getting even, retaliating	Forgiving, turning the other cheek
Accumulating, getting	Giving, sharing

Explore this question among the group members: In order to be an effective counter-community, what changes need to be made by our local church?

8. Another mark of the church as a counter-community is that its origin and life are rooted in God's continuous activity and promises. Through public worship, the sacraments, study of Scripture, fasting and abstinence, the church maintains its unique identity. Both doctrine and discipline are kept vibrant and dynamic. Remind class members that the General Rules are to be seen as responses to beliefs and doctrines, not as means of earning salvation or proving worth. Attendance upon the ordinances keeps us in touch with the affirmations and the grace that keeps the rules and the small groups in the context of God's continuing action on our behalf.

9. Close with either "An Order for Morning Praise and Prayer" (pages 876–78) or "An Order for Evening Praise and Prayer" (pages 878–79) in *The United Methodist Hymnal.*

---

[1]From *Principles of Biomedical Ethics,* by Tom L. Beauchamp and James F. Childress (Oxford University Press, 1979), pages 98–131.
[2] From *Principles of Biomedical Ethics,* pages 135–64.
[3] From *Biblical Ethics and Social Change,* by Stephen Charles Mott (Oxford University Press, 1982), pages 128–42.

A CREATIVE TENSION

Purpose of This Session:
To help adults see the difference between doctrinal standards, on one hand, and our theological task, on the other.

Goals of This Session:
1. To distinguish between doctrinal standards and theological exploration and the necessity of both.
2. To identify the various components of responsible and creative theological exploration.
3. To demonstrate that both doctrinal standards and theological inquiry are rooted in Scripture.
4. To equip adults to evaluate their own doctrinal standards and theological quest.

GROUNDING IN SCRIPTURE

The Bible reveals a God who can be known but who is beyond our total comprehension. God is present within specific places and times, but God cannot be confined to those places and times. God is described in words and hymns and creeds, but God shatters all idols, whether they be made of stone or gold or language.

The account of the call of Moses is typical of the Bible's portrayal of God (Exodus 3:1-15). God called to Moses out of the mystery of a burning bush. Moses, convinced but confused, asked for the Mysterious One's name. "God said to Moses, 'I AM WHO I AM'" (3:14). Or the name may be translated "I AM WHAT I AM" or "I WILL BE WHAT I WILL BE." In other words, the Mysterious One remains a mystery but is known in experience. Although Moses experienced the presence of God and the divine purposes were

revealed to him, the revelations were always shrouded in mystery (Exodus 19:16-19; 24:15-18; 34:5).

Isaiah 40:12-31 protrays a God who is known but who is beyond knowing. The writer describes God as transcendent:

"Have you not known? Have you not
   heard? . . . .
It is he who sits above the circle of the earth,
   and its inhabitants are like grasshoppers;
who stretches out the heavens like a curtain,
   and spreads them like a tent to live in;
who brings princes to naught,
   and makes the rulers of the earth as
   nothing" (40:21-23).

God transcends time and space but chooses to work within history.

The New Testament builds upon the revelation of the Old Testament. It affirms the essential beliefs of the Old Testament while bearing witness to God's continuing revelation. The New Testament writers reinterpreted and reapplied the Old Testament in the light of God's revelation in Jesus Christ.

Jesus described his own relationship to the affirmations of the past in these words: "Do not think that I have come to abolish but to fulfill" (Matthew 5:17). Yet in fulfilling them, Jesus expanded them and gave them new application.

The Bible is itself the supreme evidence that the theological task is critical and constructive, individual and communal, contextual and incarnational, and speculative and practical. The Bible interprets and builds upon its own unfolding revelation. Its message comes to individuals, but those individuals are products of the community's faith and experience. Amos, for example, is a lone prophetic voice crying against the injustices of the Israelites. Yet Amos's vision of justice grew out of the community's heritage as a covenant people, and his purpose was the reform and redemption of the community.

The books of the Bible arose in particular situations in response to specific and timely problems. At the same time, they proclaim timeless insights and transforming truths. The overarching purpose is incarnational, that is, that the divine Word will become flesh in the individual and the community. Paul's letters, each of which arose in response to the needs of particular congregations, become God's words to all congregations. Though the context in which 1 Corinthians 13 was first written may be different from the context of our congregations, its message transcends its original context; and its meaning is not fully known until it becomes embodied in persons.

The Bible itself, then, provides the foundation for the nature of our theological task. The Bible reveals a God who can be known and yet who cannot be contained in any experiences or in any formulations. Therefore, the Bible interprets and reinterprets past formulations and affirmations in the light of God's continuing self-disclosure amid emerging history. The Bible provides doctrinal standards and challenges those who take it seriously to engage in continued theological inquiry and exploration.

WHAT THE *DISCIPLINE* SAYS
(*Discipline*, ¶ 104; student book, pages 42–54)

Doctrinal Standards and Theological Inquiry

The theological statement approved by the 1972 General Conference emphasized pluralism. Many pastors and laypersons incorrectly interpreted pluralism to mean doctrinal relativism. Some people assumed that The United Methodist Church had no doctrines, only theological guidelines (Scripture, tradition, reason, experience). Indifference to doctrine resulted.

A major contribution of the theological statement in the current *Discipline* is its distinction between doctrinal standards and theological

exploration or inquiry. Doctrine represents the communal formulations of the essential elements or characteristics of the faith. The Articles of Religion and the Confession of Faith, for example, are formulations of basic beliefs or affirmations agreed upon by the community. Though the language and imagery must be interpreted, they define the essential categories or concepts of the faith.

Doctrines provide a framework and parameters for understanding the faith and exploring its meaning. Dr. Thomas Langford suggests a helpful analogy: "Doctrine is like a house that a religious communion already inhabits. It represents a communal agreement about what is essential to and characteristic of their faith." Theological inquiry, on the other hand, "is the proposal of blueprints for extending the house. Often individually drawn, these blueprints represent creative efforts to suggest new construction which will make the home more welcoming or adequate."[1]

Doctrine represents theological conclusions that the church has reached. Theological inquiry represents the church's attempt to interpret, expand, and apply those conclusions. Both doctrine and theology are essential to the life of the church.

Theology Contains Inevitable Tension

Theology lives with some inevitable tension and incompleteness. Theology, by its very nature, seeks to explore that which transcends past and present formulations and categories of experience. Doctrines and theological formulations never totally capture the God they affirm. Since the human mind cannot fully grasp God, and human language cannot precisely describe God, and human personality cannot experience the totality of God, the work of theology is always inadequate and incomplete.

The church and individuals are tempted to remove the tension in theology by two means. On one hand, the tension may be removed by choosing doctrinal rigidity and dogmatic creeds and resisting all theological exploration. Beliefs become fixed and sheltered from critical evaluation. Doubt becomes the enemy of faith. Faith is reduced to uncritical assent to prescribed beliefs. Doctrines tend to become idols made of language. The task of theology is limited to passing on unchanging dogma to the next generation.

The other means of removing the tension is to assume a stance of indifference and relativism. That leads to uncritical acceptance of diverse views and interpretations. In the name of tolerance, theology is reduced to a mere mental skill game in which one opinion is as valid as another. Serious grappling with the reality and purpose of the Holy Ones fades into apathy and theological illiteracy.

Theology must keep the creative tension alive and avoid both doctrinal rigidity and doctrinal indifference if it is to fulfill its purpose of interpreting the nature, purposes, and presence of the One who transcends all understandings and experiences. The theological statement defines the nature of the ongoing task of theology in helpful ways.

Our Theological Task:
Critical and Constructive

Expressions of faith, doctrines, and beliefs are to be evaluated and tested with the tools of reason, analysis, and love. The formulations of the past have to be reviewed in light of new discoveries. For example, the perception of the universe and the laws of nature presupposed in the Bible are vastly different from the understanding of creation held by modern science. The church must constantly find new ways to share the abiding truth of the Bible in categories and language compatible with the discoveries of science.

Contemporary issues, values, and philosophies require critical evaluation in the light of timeless truth, as surely as ancient beliefs must be evaluated in the light of contemporary discoveries. The mistaken assumption that modern technology and contemporary ideas have made ancient truths irrelevant or inferior is widely held in the secular world.

A few years ago I attended a conference of engineers, technologists, and scientists. One session was entitled "Ethics and Technology." The keynote speaker was Dr. Roger L. Shinn, then professor of ethics at Union Theological Seminary in New York. During a panel discussion after Dr. Shinn's address, a scientist

remarked that technology and science have advanced beyond the ethical insights of the world's religions. He said, in effect, that the ethical and moral principles of the past are irrelevant. Dr. Shinn acknowledged that the ethical principles of the past must be reinterpreted in light of new issues. He went on to say, however, that it is as presumptuous to assume that the modern world has outgrown the ethics of Moses and Jesus as it is to assume that modern literature has made Shakespeare irrelevant.

Dr. Shinn affirmed the critical and constructive nature of theology. Each generation, indeed each person, must seek to evaluate the past and build upon its wisdom and revelation. The United Methodist Church affirms that God's revelation continues and that we must remain open to new insights and new manifestations of the divine presence.

Our Theological Task:
Individual and Communal

Each individual, lay and ordained, has the responsibility to grapple critically and constructively with the nature, reality, and activity of God. Thinking theologically about every aspect of life is a task shared by all Christians, not just professional theologians or clergy. Methodism has always placed emphasis on the role of the laity in interpreting and sharing the faith. Wesley's use of lay pastors to preach and teach illustrates the shared nature of the theological task.

Doctrinal Standards and Our Theological Task is the product of a shared effort by laity and clergy, professional theologians and lay members of local churches. The Theological Study Committee consisted of laymen, laywomen, local pastors, bishops, and theology professors. The committee spent three years in prayer, study, discussion, and debate before writing the document presented to the General Conference. The General Conference legislative committee was made up of an equal number of laypersons and clergy; and the members spent sixty hours debating, altering, and finalizing the document.

Although individuals—lay and clergy, professional and nonprofessional—have responsibility to do the work of theology, that work takes place within community. Individual theological exploration is subject to the discipline and accountability of the broader community of faith. No one person determines what is authentic Christian doctrine or belief. Rather, each person's interpretation must receive the evaluation and scrutiny of others. Through dialogue and mutual searching, the truth and reality of God emerge.

Our Theological Task: Contextual and Incarnational

Theological reflection and exploration are never done in a vacuum. They emerge within a cultural, historical, and personal context. Particular circumstances influence how persons experience and perceive God. Images of God inevitably reflect the culture and experiences of the persons trying to describe the Transcendent One. For example, an agricultural culture naturally conceives of God as shepherd or vinedresser. Or a nation ruled by a monarchy naturally conceives of God as king or ruler. A patriarchal society likely describes God in masculine language.

Further, the life situations of particular persons of faith influence their theology. Oppressed persons and victims of injustice and violence tend to see God in terms of liberation, freedom, and victory. On the other hand, politically free and economically secure persons picture God primarily in terms of personal comforter and champion of the status quo.

United Methodists affirm the validity and necessity of openness to diverse contextual expressions of the divine reality and presence. We affirm the contributions to the church's understanding of God made in recent years by those brothers and sisters who speak out of the context of racial, political, and economic oppression. We further affirm the enrichment of our understanding and experience of God brought by those whose context causes them to insist that God is more than can be conceptualized in traditional male images.

Theological inquiry is contextual and incarnational. God's supreme mode of self-revelation, the Incarnation in Jesus Christ, is the foundation for all Christian theological inquiry. As John's Gospel affirms, "The Word [the *Logos*,

the wisdom, the mind of God] became flesh and lived among us" (John 1:14). God continues to meet us in the flesh and blood of the real world and real people.

Our Theological Task: Practical and Relevant

The United Methodist tradition is *practical divinity*. Theology in the biblical and the Wesleyan tradition seeks openness to the presence and purposes of God amid the realities of everyday life. It seeks to know and do God's will in the boardroom and the bedroom, the laboratory and the lecture hall, the voting booth and the marketplace, the playground and the sports arena, the sanctuary and the slum. In short, the ultimate purpose of theology and doctrine is to support holy living.

A single parent, divorced for three years, attended a seminar for singles at a local United Methodist church. She called the pastor and said, "I want to know more about what your church believes. Your church seems to be concerned with life, not just with religion." She was learning that the church is concerned with religion's impact on life, that theology is practical.

A world-known nuclear physicist, a nominal church member, was invited to attend a dialogue between United Methodist bishops and scientists and engineers involved in nuclear weapons research and production. After the dialogue, he said to the pastor, "It never occurred to me to make a connection between the church and the laboratory. I realize now that I have kept my religion and my science in separate compartments." That physicist now is raising new questions about both his science and his religion.

Conclusion

Theology, for John Wesley and his United Methodist heirs, has always been an essential part of the church's mission and of the individual's responsibility. Failure to take seriously the ongoing task of discerning and living out the nature and purposes of God is to forfeit the church's identity and mission.

Pastors and laypersons frequently hide from the task by shrugging their shoulders and saying, "I'm no theologian." Everyone in the whole church, however, is a theologian. Laypersons and clergy, professional academics and nonprofessionals, all share the awesome and challenging responsibility to discern and live in the presence of God. Fulfilling the theological task in a spirit of humility before God, openness to one another, and commitment to living the truth in love will enable The United Methodist Church to minister prophetically and redemptively in a world filled with God's presence and claimed by God's purposes.

THE SESSION PLAN

1. It is important that participants distinguish between doctrine and theological inquiry. To illustrate graphically Dr. Langford's analogy of doctrine as a house, obtain building blocks from the church nursery. Ask class members to write on adhesive labels key words or phrases representing the essential doctrines in the Articles of Religion and the Confession of Faith. Read aloud the labels as you tape them to the blocks. Then arrange the blocks in some fashion to represent a house and ask these questions: Do you agree with the placement of the blocks? Which doctrines should form the foundation? The roof? The windows? Why?

Point out that the blocks represent the essential material for the theological house. The discussion of the placement of the blocks (the role of the doctrines) is theological inquiry.

Expand this activity by asking how the design or structure would need alteration if, for example, the house were to be located in an earthquake or flood zone. Would you add any blocks? If so, what? Where? This is theological exploration.

Ask this further question: Does the house fully contain the reality, nature, and activity of God? To limit God to the confines of the "house of doctrines" would be to make the house synonymous with God, which is idolatry. Adding on to the house, redesigning it to fit its environment and in response to new threats or conditions, requires several tools and resources. That leads us into consideration of the nature of our theological task.

2. The Bible reflects the dual nature of our theological task. The Bible contains basic affir-

mations about God, and one of those affirmations is that God cannot be contained totally in doctrines. One must remain open to further revelation while holding fast to revelation already received. Review for the group the material in "Grounding in Scripture" in this leader's guide.

3. Write on the top of a chalkboard or sheet of paper "Our Theological Task." Underneath that heading, write the key words used in the *Discipline* to describe that ask:
   • critical and constructive
   • individual and incarnational
   • contextual and incarnational
   • practical

4. Now return to the image of the house. Talk about the nature of our theological task in terms of that imagery. For example, in order to live and move about in the house, one must understand it and have confidence in its structural integrity. To expand it or update it, one must be both critical (evaluate it) and constructive (build upon the past by analyzing the structure and design in light of new materials available and new threats or demands). Additions and alterations involve many persons—architects, skilled workers, laborers, and so on. Remodeling the house is, in reality, a collective effort.

In the same way, the theological task involves the whole community of faith—professional theologians, pastors, laity, bishops, and so on. The task is individual and communal. The construction is done in a particular place. The design of the house, the materials used, the type of heating and cooling installed are influenced by the environment (context). Construction involves people working together, sharing expertise and experience. And the house has little relevance apart from the living persons who dwell in it (incarnational).

Not all houses are of equal value. It is possible to build houses that no one can inhabit; or, a house may be beautiful but unable to withstand wind, rain, freezing cold, and storms; or, one might simply build dollhouses, which aren't real houses at all. So it is with theology. For

Wesley, however, "practical divinity" was the rule. Theology is to promote the spiritual health of the community and individuals. It is practical.

5. Ask class members to spend a few minutes reflecting on their own "theological house." Ask these questions: What are the doctrines that you hold firm? How has your understanding of those doctrines changed since you were a child or a youth? What areas remain unfinished? Invite volunteers to report the fruits of their reflection.

6. Read to the class this statement from the *Discipline:* "Theology is our effort to reflect upon God's gracious action in our lives. In response to the love of Christ, we desire to be drawn into a deeper relationship with the 'author and perfecter of our faith.' Our theological explorations seek to give expression to the mysterious reality of God's presence, peace,

and power in the world" (¶ 104; student book, page 42). Theology is the vital business of all who seek to be the people of God.

7. Close with the following prayer for motivation, insight, and courage to be about our theological task:

"O God, you are beyond our comprehension, and yet you make yourself known within our experience and thought. Your presence extends to the farthest reaches of space, and yet you are present with the least and lowest of your creation. Help us, O God, to understand and commit ourselves to that which is timeless. At the same time, keep us open to new insights into your purposes, fresh experiences of your gracious presence, and clearer visions of your new heaven and new earth. Through Jesus Christ we pray. Amen."

[1]From "Conciliar Theology: A Report," by Thomas A. Langford, in *Quarterly Review* (Summer 1989), page 9.

THEOLOGICAL GUIDELINES

Purpose of This Session:

To help adults understand how Scripture, tradition, reason, and experience can and should serve as guidelines (sources and criteria) for engaging in our theological task.

Goals of This Session:

1. To help adults get a better grasp of the interrelationship of Scripture, tradition, experience, and reason as both sources and criteria for theology.
2. To encourage participants to discuss the claim that, among the four guidelines for theology, Scripture is primary in matters of faith.

GROUNDING IN SCRIPTURE

The Bible is both the primary source and the primary criterion of knowledge of God. The Bible is United Methodism's preeminent guideline for evaluating doctrine and for exploring the continuing revelation of God's nature and purposes. The Bible affirms God's action in history (tradition), God's presence within human existence (experience), and God's gift of human understanding (reason).

Holy Scripture bears testimony to its own primacy in matters of faith. We depend upon the Bible as a record of God's involvement in human history and in all of creation—from the call of Abraham to the deliverance from Egyptian slavery and the establishment of the nation, from the Incarnation in Jesus the Christ to the promise of a new heaven and a new earth when God's victory over sin and death will be complete. The Bible introduces us to the God who brought creation into being and stamped the divine image into human potential, and

who relentlessly seeks to restore the divine image in the human family.

Scripture is the indispensable core of God's self-revelation. Without Scripture, tradition would contain a scant deposit of revelation. Experience would be thin and would have no central moorings by which to be judged and challenged. Reason without Scripture might provide intimations of God, but it could just as easily lead us into the darkness of stuffy rationalism. Tradition, experience, and reason may illumine and be illumined by Scripture, but they do not displace Scripture.

The Bible affirms tradition as a source and criterion for divine revelation. Throughout the Old Testament the people are admonished "to remember." Memory was a source of renewal and guidance. Deuteronomy, for example, became important during the collapse of Israel. Deuteronomy is a warning to the nation of the consequences of ignoring the tradition of God's covenant. It is filled with calls to remember God's mighty acts of deliverance and God's commandments and ordinances. The prophets contended that the collapse of the nation resulted from the failure to remember the covenant. When the nation fell, hope was kindled by recalling God's promises.

Jesus demonstrated the importance of memory and tradition. On the night before his death, he took bread, blessed it, and gave it to his disciples and said, "Do this in remembrance of me" (Luke 22:19; 1 Corinthians 11:24). His own familiarity with the traditions of Judaism is evident throughout the Gospels, and he frequently appealed to tradition to answer his critics (Matthew 15:1-9; 22:34-40; Mark 12:28-34; Luke 20:17-18, 33-44). In his final hours on the cross he found strength in a hymn of his tradition, Psalm 22 (Matthew 27:46).

Paul makes use of the traditions of his Hebrew heritage in interpreting his experience of God's redemptive and reconciling acts in Jesus Christ. For example, in the Letter to the Romans, Paul makes more than eighty explicit or implicit references to Old Testament passages. He makes use of Psalms, wisdom writings, the prophets, as well as the Pentateuch (the first five books of the Old Testament). In other words, the whole range of his sacred tradition informed and instructed his experience of and faith in Jesus Christ.

Other books of the New Testament represent a building upon the traditions of the past. Hebrews uses tradition to define faith (Hebrews 11). The Book of Revelation forges the imagery of the new heaven and the new earth out of the tradition of Ezekiel and Isaiah (*see* Revelation 21; Isaiah 66:22; 25:8; 35:10; 43:19; 55:1; Ezekiel 37:27; 40:2; 48:30-35).

The Bible clearly affirms the importance of experience as a source of revelation and a tool for evaluating revelation. The Bible knows no revelation of God apart from the historical life situation of individuals and communities. God's self-disclosure takes place within the experiences of persons. The Hebrew nation traces its origin to God's act of deliverance from Egyptian slavery (Exodus 1–14). From the experience of the Exodus the Hebrews interpreted Creation's origin and their own ancestors.

Paul's experience on the Damascus road changed his understanding of God and the means of salvation (Acts 9:1-19; 22:3-16; 26:9-18). The apostles' experience of the risen Christ freed them from despair and failure and sent them out of the hiding place to proclaim the good news of God's triumph over sin and death (Matthew 28; Luke 24; John 20–21). The experience of the gift of God's Spirit at Pentecost brought the church into being (Acts 2). The experience of persecution gave rise to John's vision of God's final victory as described in the Book of Revelation.

Finally, the Bible also reflects the role of reason in matters of faith. It is no accident that the Bible contains what scholars call *wisdom literature.* Proverbs, Ecclesiastes, and Job tackle tough intellectual questions that continue to baffle the best minds. Although the answers may be incomplete, they demonstrate that the human mind is a fertile field for the seeds of God's presence and truth.

Jesus' teachings require thoughtful reflection and careful analysis. He used the method of story, or parable, which requires the hearers to put themselves mentally and imaginatively in the stories. Jesus often responded to inquiries by asking questions. In so doing, he prodded people to reflect critically on their perceptions, experiences, and traditions.

John's Gospel uses the term *Logos* to describe the Incarnation (John 1:1-14), combining the Hebrew and Greek understandings of the term. *Logos* means wisdom, reason, mind. God's wisdom, God's reason, God's thoughts became flesh in Jesus Christ.

Paul was one of the towering intellects of the ancient world. He was well schooled in Hebrew and Greek thought, and he employed his intellect in interpreting and defending the faith. For example, to the intellectuals of Athens Paul appealed to philosophy as a point of identification (Acts 17:22-31). His letters reflect his exceptional use of reason in explaining and defending what he knew through his tradition and through his experience of God's grace in Jesus Christ.

United Methodism's emphasis on the Bible, tradition, experience, and reason as sources of revelation and tools for interpreting that revelation is firmly grounded in Scripture.

WHAT THE *DISCIPLINE* SAYS
(*Discipline,* ¶ 104; student book, pages 42–54)

A new United Methodist was asked by a co-worker for a justification of infant baptism. The recent convert responded with embarrassment, "I don't know, but I will find out." The colleague retorted, "Oh, I didn't really expect you to know. I've never met a Methodist who knew what he or she believed, and they don't usually have anything other than their own opinion to go on."

On the contrary, United Methodists have a "marrow" of beliefs and doctrines. And we have clearly identified guidelines for interpreting, expanding, and altering those affirmations. A core of doctrine and guidelines for theological inquiry are deeply rooted in the Wesleyan heritage.

John Wesley used the accepted Anglican guidelines—Scripture, "Christian antiquity," and reason. To these three, he added "experience." These four guidelines were affirmed and emphasized in the theological statement adopted by the 1972 General Conference.

Between 1972 and the mid-1980s the guidelines seem to have been misinterpreted by many clergy and laity. One clergy was overheard to say to a prospective United Methodist, "We don't have doctrines that you must affirm. We have four guidelines by which you determine your own beliefs." The result of such an interpretation of the 1972 statement was that the guidelines replaced the doctrines and tended to promote an indifference to doctrine.

Also, many people interpreted the four guidelines to be equal and independent of one another. Although the 1972 statement clearly affirmed the primacy of Scripture, many interpreters relegated the Bible to a position equal with reason, tradition, and experience.

Furthermore, some interpreters of the guidelines treated them as independent of one another, assuming that one could be employed without the other. The 1988 statement affirms that each guidelines requires the others and that they cannot be segmented without distorting them all.

Interrelatedness of the Guidelines

Exploring the reality, presence, and purposes of God involves the use of Scripture, reason, experience, and tradition. In a sense, the four cannot be isolated any more than personhood can be segmented into body, mind, relationships, and history. Dissecting a person into such components destroys the meaning of personhood. Scripture, reason, tradition, and experience are so interrelated and mutually dependent as sources of God's revelation that to isolate one from the other is to distort them all.

Scripture, through primary, is also part of the tradition and experience that are understood and perceived through reason. Reason itself is fueled by experience and tradition. Scripture informs reason, molds and shapes experience, and interprets tradition. All four enable us to perceive and know God, as the mind, the body, and the emotions relate us to the world of which we are part.

Scripture, tradition, reason, and experience are criteria by which we evaluate doctrine, affirmations, and revelation. They are tools for perceiving God's revelation and avenues of God's revelation. God comes to us in Scripture, in history, and through reason and experience. Thoughts and feelings, as surely as history and Scripture, are roadways over which the Transcendent One comes and makes the eternal known.

The diagram on page 75 illustrates the interdependence of the four criteria and sources.[1]

The Primacy of Scripture

Much discussion before and during the 1988 General Conference centered around the primacy of Scripture. The question, for United Methodists, has never been whether or not the Bible is primary in matters of faith. The issue in recent times has been the definition of *primacy* and the source of the Bible's authority.

Albert Outler affirms, "Wesley's point of departure was always Holy Scripture, understood according to the 'analogy of faith' (i.e., its general sense) and as 'the standing revelation' in the Christian church throughout her long history."[2]

Wesley, as early as 1729, referred to himself as "a man of one book." Article V of the Articles of Religion and Article IV of the Confession of Faith clearly affirm that the Holy Scripture contains all things necessary for salvation. Wesley's own life was so immersed in Scripture that its stories and language were as familiar to him as his own life's experience and his native language.

United Methodists, however, have understood the authority of Scripture to be grounded not in its verbal inspiration or factual accuracy but in the Living Word to which it bears witness. Primacy is not to be interpreted linearly or hierarchically. It is God's revelation, supremely given in Christ, that is primary. The Bible is the principal testimony to that revelation. It serves for us the role that John the Baptist served for the Messiah. He

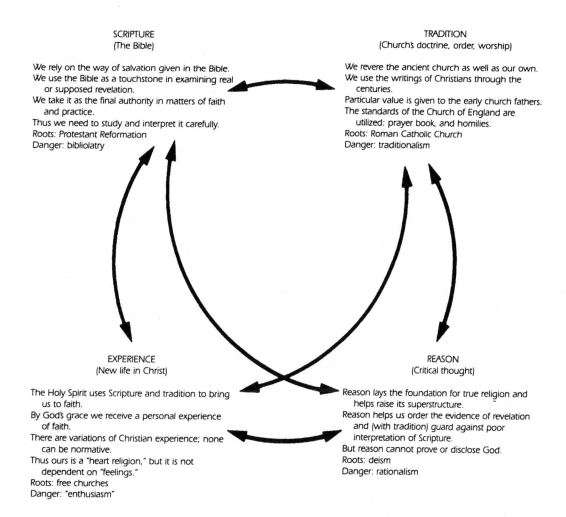

SCRIPTURE
(The Bible)

We rely on the way of salvation given in the Bible.
We use the Bible as a touchstone in examining real
 or supposed revelation.
We take it as the final authority in matters of faith
 and practice.
Thus we need to study and interpret it carefully.
Roots: Protestant Reformation
Danger: bibliolatry

TRADITION
(Church's doctrine, order, worship)

We revere the ancient church as well as our own.
We use the writings of Christians through the
 centuries.
Particular value is given to the early church fathers.
The standards of the Church of England are
 utilized: prayer book, and homilies.
Roots: Roman Catholic Church
Danger: traditionalism

EXPERIENCE
(New life in Christ)

The Holy Spirit uses Scripture and tradition to bring
 us to faith.
By God's grace we receive a personal experience
 of faith.
There are variations of Christian experience; none
 can be normative.
Thus ours is a "heart religion," but it is not
 dependent on "feelings."
Roots: free churches
Danger: "enthusiasm"

REASON
(Critical thought)

Reason lays the foundation for true religion and
 helps raise its superstructure.
Reason helps us order the evidence of revelation
 and (with tradition) guard against poor
 interpretation of Scripture.
But reason cannot prove or disclose God.
Roots: deism
Danger: rationalism

bore witness to the light but was not to be equated with the light. The Bible's authority is due to its remarkable capacity to bear witness to the light of God's self-disclosure.

Although Wesley referred to himself as a man of one book, he believed that anyone who read the Bible only did not properly understand the Bible. He considered the Bible sufficient in matters of faith, but he never gave any indication that he considered Holy Scripture to be sufficient for all matters. He read widely in literature, the science of his day, history, and other disciplines. Wesley and his successors have considered the Bible as primary in matters of faith. They have not seen it as a primary source for the study of science or world history.

Taking the Bible seriously is not the same as taking the Bible literally. Serious reading of Scripture requires taking its historical and literary setting into consideration. It involves enter-

ing the world of the Bible, struggling with its language and symbols, its literary devices and cultural reflections.

Wesley's five principles of interpretation are worthy of use by the modern church:

1. Believers should accustom themselves to the biblical language, thus to the "general sense" of the Scripture as a whole.
2. Scriptures are to be read as a whole, with the expectation that the clearer texts may be relied upon to illuminate the obscurer ones.
3. One's exegesis is to be guided, always in the first instance, by the literal sense, unless that appears to lead to consequences that are either irrational or unworthy of God's character as "pure, unbounded love."
4. All moral commands in Scripture are also "covered promises," since God never commands the impossible and his

grace is always efficacious in every faithful will.

5. The historical experience of the church, though fallible, is the better judge overall of Scripture's meaning than later interpreters are likely to be, especially their own. Thus, radical novelty is to be eschewed.[3]

A lively doctrine of the Holy Spirit prevented the United Methodist traditions from moving to biblical literalism or infallibility. Scholars agree that Wesley's strong conviction of the authority of Scripture in matters of faith was rooted in his view that the whole of the Bible contained a consistent theme. As Timothy L. Smith makes clear, according to Wesley, "the living center of every part of inspired Scripture was the call to be holy, and the promise of grace to answer that call."[4] Through the inspiration of the Holy Spirit, Scripture makes known the holiness of God and challenges and empowers the faithful to live out that holiness in their lives. Therein lies the authority and primacy of Scripture as source and criterion for our continuing theological task.

Tradition as a Source and Criterion

The Bible speaks of a God whose presence and purposes are known in historical events. The Exodus of the Hebrews from Egyptian slavery, the giving of the Law on Sinai, the building of the Hebrew nation, the Assyrian and Babylonian captivity and subsequent restoration, the Incarnation in Jesus Christ, Pentecost, and the establishing of the church—these are key events in the church's tradition. The hymns and affirmations of the psalms and the prayers and liturgies of Judaism and the early church form part of the storehouse of tradition. The writings of early church leaders, including those that are part of the New Testament and many extrabiblical sources, contain revelatory insights that cannot be ignored by those who seek to know God. Neither can we ignore the historic creeds and life stories of pilgrims of faith through the ages.

Theological inquiry is formed by and builds upon the cumulative experience of the church through the ages. The theological statement says, "The theological task does not start anew in each age or each person. Christianity does not leap from New Testament times to the present as though nothing were to be learned from that great cloud of witnesses in between" (*Discipline*, ¶ 104; student book, page 47).

Tradition reflects the diversity of experiences, revelations, and understandings. The church's history is woven out of a multifaceted, multicultural fabric, with threads emerging from many diverse peoples. Appreciation of diversity in theological perspective is part of the church's tradition, traceable to the Bible itself.

Evaluating the faith of the church or the individual, then, requires a reading of history. How does a particular belief fit with the mainstream of church history? A wholistic perspective on history is as important as a wholistic perspective on the Bible. Otherwise, we fall victims to the fallacy of selective history, which is similar to prooftexting in the use of Scripture.

Tradition, though diverse, also reflects a continuity of experience and revelation. Ignoring the continuity of tradition's themes and insights in our continuing theological quest is as absurd as attempting to face each new day with no memory of the past.

According to the theological statement, "Tradition acts as a measure of validity and propriety for a community's faith insofar as it represents a consensus of faith" (*Discipline*, ¶ 104; student book, page 48). Theological inquiry includes this question: Do the traditional affirmations make sense in the light of contemporary experience and knowledge? Tradition, in other words, is dynamic and cumulative; and our theological work is contributing to the tradition.

Individual novelty in theological matters must be checked for validity against the broader tradition of the Christian community. Again, the primary source or criterion must be Scripture.

When someone wrote John Wesley early in 1739 appealing to churchly tradition, Wesley responded, "If by catholic principles you mean any other than scriptural, they weigh nothing with me. I allow no other rule, whether of faith or practice, than the Holy Scriptures." Yet

Wesley also urged ministers of the Church of England to "acquire a 'knowledge of the Fathers,' because they were 'the most authentic commentators on Scripture, as being both nearest the fountain, and eminently endued with the Spirit by whom all Scripture is given.' "[5]

Experience as a Source and Criterion

Wesley's understanding of *experience* as a source and criterion was twofold. First, it refers to the personal assurance of God's justifying, pardoning grace. " 'New life in Christ' is what we as United Methodists mean when we speak of 'Christian experience' " (*Discipline*, ¶ 104; student book, page 49). Theological exploration in the Wesleyan tradition involves examining our experience of God's justifying, pardoning grace. And it implies an openness to fresh experiences of the transforming presence of God through the Holy Spirit.

Experience to Wesley also refers to the commonsense experience of the individual and the community. Experiences of the individual and the entire human family are sources of insight and revelation and criteria by which insights and revelation are evaluated. Our life experiences influence how we perceive God, how we come to know God's grace, and how we express God's grace in everyday living.

Experience, like tradition, is diverse. Oppressed peoples experience God as liberator. Sorrowing persons seek a God who comforts and sustains. Women, out of their own experience, are helping the church recover dimensions of the divine reality that tend to be lost when only males interpret images of God.

Experience is both a locus of God's revelation and a means of evaluating revelation. Divine grace and presence are known in the midst of all life. There is a transcendent dimension to all experience as the Holy Spirit ever works within life's routines. God's presence permeates all existence. Sensitivity and openness to the One in whom we live and move and have our being are part of our theological task.

"Practical divinity" leads us to ask of all theological affirmations, Does it ring true in my experience? If it does, experience has helped to validate the affirmation. If it does not ring true to our experience, it may either be a challenge to our experience or a challenge to the validity of the affirmation.

Lest personal experience be made ultimate, however, experience must be interpreted and evaluated by Scripture, tradition, and reason. Without Scripture, tradition, and reason, the faith is reduced to private, subjective experiences, and God becomes the champion of selfish interests and a source of personal and communal gratification.

Reason as a Source and Criterion

Wesley used reason as a tool for clarifying and interpreting Scripture, tradition, and experience. A fundamental principle of the Methodists, Wesley wrote in 1768 in a sharply worded reply to a theologian at Cambridge University, is "that to renounce reason is to renounce religion" for "all irrational religion is false religion."[6]

Reason too is both a source of revelation and a criterion for receiving and evaluating revelation. The role of reason is made explicit in the following paragraph added to the theological statement by the General Conference Legislative Committee: "Since all truth is from God, efforts to discern the connections between revelation and reason, faith and science, grace and nature, are useful endeavors in developing credible and communicable doctrine. We seek nothing less than a total view of reality that is decisively informed by the promises and imperatives of the Christian gospel" (*Discipline*, ¶ 104; student book, page 50).

The human mind is one of God's most precious gifts, and its use as a means of loving God is an expression of responsible stewardship. Anti-intellectualism has been a temptation for some segments of the church. Resistance to an educated clergy is one segment of the American church's tradition. The temptation to denigrate reason must be resisted if United Methodists are to be true to their heritage and if they are to be a relevant voice in the contemporary world.

On the other hand, United Methodists also must resist the temptation to make reason an idol. A caution from Wesley in a sermon entitled "The Case of Reason Impartially Considered" is helpful: "Let reason do all that reason can: employ it as far as it will go. But at the same time acknowledge it is utterly incapable of giving either faith, or hope, or love; and consequently of producing either real virtue or substantial happiness. Expect these from a higher source, even from the Father of the spirits of all flesh."[7]

Conclusion

The theological statement summarizes the sources and criteria of our theological task: "In theological reflection, the resources of tradition, experience, and reason are integral to our study of Scripture without displacing Scripture's primacy for faith and practice. These four sources—each making distinctive contributions, yet all finally working together—guide our quest as United Methodists for a vital and appropriate Christian witness" (*Discipline*, ¶ 104; student book, page 51).

Theological inquiry may *begin* from any of the four guidelines. A friend who is a scientist began her faith journey when she confronted the profound mystery of the universe and the interrelatedness of all creation. She began to read the Bible, not as a textbook of science, but as an affirmation of faith in a Creator. There she was led into new directions of meaning and purpose. Her pilgrimage has included a discovery of the mystics and a growing appreciation of their sense of mystery before the transcendent. She is now a member of The United Methodist Church. She helps other United Methodists, who began their pilgrimage in Scripture or tradition, to broaden and deepen their understanding of God through the use of experience and reason.

In the contemporary world where conflicting religions and secular ideologies vie for people's loyalty, The United Methodist Church's theological criteria and sources provide reliable tools and resources. With Scripture occupying central focus, United Methodists affirm tradition, experience, and reason as necessary sources of God's revelation and as indispensable tools with which to evaluate that revelation.

THE SESSION PLAN

1. Begin the session by retelling either the illustration of the United Methodist who was asked to justify infant baptism (page 73 of this leader's guide) or a similar incident from your own experience. Ask this question: How would you respond to the person who charged, "I've never met a Methodist who knew what he or she believed"? After a few responses, ask this further question: Why do you think United Methodists are sometimes perceived as having no firm doctrinal positions?

Briefly review from Session 8 the distinction between doctrine and theological exploration or inquiry. Point out that an emphasis on guidelines without an accompanying emphasis on the "marrow" or core doctrines may lead to indifference toward doctrine.

2. Show the class the diagram on page 75 of this leader's guide or copy it on chalkboard or a large sheet of paper. Explain the interaction of the four criteria according to the diagram. Read aloud or paraphrase the material under "What the *Discipline* Says" on pages 73–78 in this leader's guide.

3. Select an important belief and evaluate it in terms of the four criteria, using the diagram from this leader's guide or the drawing on chalkboard or paper. One possible issue is the mode of baptism. The practice of baptism is affirmed in the Bible, and the disciples were directed by Jesus to baptize "in the name of the Father and of the Son and of the Holy Spirit" (Matthew 28:19). We know that Jesus was baptized by John the Baptist in the Jordan River. However, the Bible does not specify the explicit mode of baptism. Tradition in Judaism and the early church provides for three modes—pouring, sprinkling, and immersion. We know that all three methods have been used for centuries. Experience and reason, then, become crucial tools. Some find that the dramatic symbolism of immersion is a profound experience of the burying of the old self and the rising of the new. Others, however, find immersion distracting from the experience of the gentle cleansing of sin or the flow of God's Spirit through pouring. Some *reason* that immersion is more compatible with the meaning of the sacrament. Others, however, argue that as a sign, the amount of

water and particular method do not alter the sign's meaning. As a result of the four criteria, The United Methodist Church allows for three modes and accepts the baptism of all churches as valid.

4. To get the study group thinking about what *primacy* of Scripture means, describe three imaginary persons who interpret the Bible in the following different ways:

• One interprets the Bible literally. He believes that the Bible is self-interpreting and that the use of commentaries is a crutch. The Bible means exactly what it says, and each part of the Bible is equally authoritative.

• A second person is a literature teacher. She views the Bible primarily as a collection of literature. She interprets the passages of the Bible with the same tools and approach that she uses to interpret a passage from Homer or Shakespeare or Keats.

• A third person is a committed Christian who believes that the Bible is God's Word but written in human words. He or she takes the Bible seriously but believes that it reflects the limitations of the culture and the language in which it was written.

Divide the class into three teams, one to represent each of the three imaginary persons. Assign one or more of these passages to each group: Genesis 1–2; Jonah 1-4; Luke 4:16-30; John 1:1-16. Invite each team to coach one team member about how to read the passage as the imaginary person would read it. After a few minutes, let the three team representatives report their interpretations.

Then ask the whole group these questions: Which position takes the primacy of Scripture most seriously? Why? Make clear that the theological statement from the 1988 General Conference is designed to chart a middle course between two extremes: (1) putting Scripture on the same level of authority as tradition, reason, and experience, and (2) raising the Bible so high that we slip into biblioatry (worshiping the Bible instead of worshiping God).

You also may ask this question: What is the difference between belief in the inerrancy of the Bible and belief in the primacy or centrality of the Bible? (As an ex-literalist, I can testify that I take the Bible more seriously now than I did as a literalist. Now I consider textual issues, its historical and literary context, its origin and development.)

5. Write on chalkboard or posterboard key phrases from Wesley's five principles of biblical interpretation (from pages 75–76 of this leader's guide). Read aloud the entire subsection in the leader's guide entitled "The Primacy of Scripture," including the five principles. Then ask group members whether they think Wesley's principles are helpful. What do group members think it means to take the Bible seriously?

6. A motion was made at General Conference that the following statement be inserted into the paragraph dealing with Scripture: "Scripture contains both authoritative witness to the Word of God and expressions of human and cultural limitation." Ask class members to give some reasons to support or to reject inclusion of the statement.

7. Retell the illustrations about the scientist who came to the faith from her experience and reason. Ask group members to describe a belief or affirmation about God that they hold for which experience or reason is the source. You as the leader may wish to talk about the role that Scripture, tradition, experience, and reason have played in your own faith development:

8. Close with the following litany:

Leader: Eternal God, you reveal yourself through the Bible, which bears witness to your ongoing work in creation, in history, in human thought and experience, and supremely in Jesus the Christ. We thank you, O God, for the Holy Scriptures; and we pray for the guidance of your Holy Spirit as we seek to interpret and live by your Word.
People: Thank you, O God, for making yourself known to us.

Leader: You, O God, have made yourself known throughout history in the lives and works of the saints and martyrs, the prophets and priests, the apostles and teachers, and through historic creeds and ancient writings, through reformers and theologians and evangelists who have gone before us. We praise you, O God, for the great cloud of witnesses who surround us; and through your Spirit enable us both to appreciate our heritage and faithfully to build upon it.

People: Thank you, O God, for making yourself known to us.

Leader: You have claimed all of life as the realm of the Divine Presence and the arena of transforming grace; and you come to us in the midst of life's sorrows and pains, its triumphs and tragedies, its challenges and relationships; and through your presence all of living becomes a means of grace. We are grateful, O God, that we are created for continuing fellowship with you, with one another, and with the world about us; and we pray for an awareness of your presence in all experience.

People: Thank you, O God, for making yourself known to us.

Leader: You, O God, are the source of all truth. You have created us with minds and the capacity to reason, and you have called us to love you with the mind as well as with the heart and the will. We thank you, O God, for the human mind and for those who have helped us to think more clearly about you and the world you are ever seeking to transform into a new heaven and a new earth.

People: Thank you, O God, for making yourself known to us.

Leader: Expand our understanding of your Word, deepen our commitment to your purposes, strengthen our love for you and for one another, and enable us to grow into the likeness of Jesus Christ, in whose name we pray. Amen.

---

[1] Diagram reprinted from *The Gospel According to Wesley*. Copyright © 1982. Discipleship Resources, P.O. Box 189, Nashville, Tennessee 37202. Reproduced by permission.

[2] From *The Works of John Wesley, Volume 1*, edited by Albert C. Outler (Abingdon Press, 1984), page 57.

[3] Excerpted and adapted from *The Works of John Wesley, Volume 1*, pages 58–59.

[4] From "John Wesley and the Wholeness of Scripture," by Timothy L. Smith, in *Interpretation*, July 1985, page 246.

[5] From "John Wesley and the Wholeness of Scripture," page 250.

[6] From "John Wesley and the Wholeness of Scripture," page 251.

[7] From *The Works of John Wesley, Volume 2*, edited by Albert C. Outler (Abingdon Press, 1985), page 600.

PERSONAL DECISION MAKING

Purpose of This Session:

To help adults learn how to think theologically about issues they personally face, drawing upon Scripture, tradition, reason, and experience as guidelines for decision making.

Goals of This Session:

1. To help participants become more adept at drawing upon Scripture, tradition, reason, and experience when facing personal issues and decisions.
2. To cultivate among adults appreciation for the theological statements as foundational for *doing* theology.

GROUNDING IN SCRIPTURE

The Bible contains the stories of persons and communities doing theology in the context of specific personal and communal situations. Scripture is the *result* of efforts by individuals and groups to understand, interpret, implement, and communicate the presence, purposes, and activity of God. That means *our* efforts to understand and shape our experiences and decisions in terms of God's reality and purpose are compatible with and mandated by Scripture.

The pivotal event in the history of Israel and in the Old Testament is the deliverance of the Hebrew slaves from Egypt. The Pentateuch, the first five books of the Old Testament, represents the theological understanding of the event and its meaning for the Hebrew people. Slavery was the personal and communal context. How were the people to understand their slavery and their subsequent freedom?

The Exodus was seen as God's mighty act on behalf of the people with whose ancestors God had entered into covenant. Their tradition included the covenant with Abraham and his descendants (Genesis 12:1-3). The experience of deliverance from slavery confirmed for them the covenant and sealed their identity as God's people.

The tradition of the Exodus and the covenant shaped the history and the self-understanding of the people of Israel. All subsequent events were interpreted in the light of that tradition. The Hebrew Scriptures, including the Law and the Prophets and the Wisdom Writings, are the products of the theology done in the light of the covenant and the Exodus. The covenant and Exodus shaped the experiences and ordered the communal life of the Hebrew people. At the same time, the people interpreted and coped with their life situations using the tradition of the covenant and Exodus. The Hebrew Scriptures were sources and criteria by which the people faced crises, interpreted life, and celebrated their relationship with God.

The comparable pivotal experience in the church's history and in the New Testament is the Christ event. The life, teachings, death, and resurrection of Jesus Christ became the source and criteria by which the early church shaped its life. Traditions developed in the form of stories about Jesus, collections of his teachings, interpretations of his life and death and resurrection. The New Testament is composed of those traditions and their implication for situations faced by individuals and by communities of faith.

The Gospels, Paul's letters, the Pastoral Letters, the apocalyptic writing of Revelation—all of the New Testament represents the early church's theology done in specific situations. Personal and community realities were shaped by the Christ event. As early Christians faced personal and community needs, they did so with the resource of God's revelation.

The entire Bible, then, is the primary casebook of persons and communities doing theology in the context of life situations. Its message transcends the original specific situations; therefore, Scripture is the central source for the continuing task of discerning and living in terms of God's presence and purposes.

The story of the encounter between Jesus and Zacchaeus, the chief tax collector of Jericho, illustrates theology being done in the face of a personal need and decision (Luke 19:1-10). The incident illustrates how the four theological guidelines come to bear upon personal life situations.

The story of Zacchaeus tells us about the importance of *experience* at two levels. First, at the level of everyday, ordinary experience, Zacchaeus must have felt that, despite his wealth, something was missing in his life. No doubt he was keenly aware that his fellow Jews resented him because he worked for the Romans. Maybe he was simply disappointed that his wealth could buy luxuries but not joy. Whatever the cause, Zacchaeus was dissatisfied enough to come looking for Jesus. Ordinary, everyday experience left Zacchaeus curious, at the very least, and perhaps flirting with hope.

At another level of experience, Zacchaeus was transformed at the core by his encounter with Jesus. Because of Jesus' welcome and acceptance, the chief tax collector knew a joy that had always before eluded him. For the first time in his adult life, he knew he was seen as a person of worth, not because of his bank account but because Jesus declared that he was worth meeting, worth taking seriously, worth redeeming.

How does *Scripture* enter into the story? Zacchaeus's promise of restitution to anyone he had wronged implies an awareness that fraud violated scriptural standards for community life. Before his encounter with Jesus, Zacchaeus chose to ignore that biblical prohibition. After his encounter with Jesus, Zacchaeus apparently felt that he was accountable to the standards in the Scriptures.

Reason as a guideline for decision making also enters into the story only implicitly. Knowing that his life was changed by meeting Jesus, and grasping intuitively that fair treatment of others was to be a characteristic of his new life, Zacchaeus leaped to the logical implication: Make restitution to those persons he had wronged. Reason alone surely would not have led him to give away his money. But reason motivated by experience and guided by Scripture did enable Zacchaeus to spin out the implication for his behavior.

It was Jesus who reclaimed *tradition* for Zacchaeus. As a despised chief tax collector, Zacchaeus must have felt alienated from his religious heritage as a Jew. Then Jesus announced, "He too is a son of Abraham" (Luke 19:9). Jesus restored Zacchaeus to his tradition as a devout Jew. Much remained to be explored and appropriated by Zacchaeus, but the door was now opened for him.

Luke used the faith quest of one person to inform and shape the faith of the broader community. The story of Zacchaeus (and every other biblical story) becomes a source and criterion by which other individuals and communities interpret and shape their lives.

Scripture undergirds and guides the ongoing theological task of persons facing personal issues and decisions. It not only describes persons doing theology, but it is the primary resource for the task. The Bible's central position in the work of Christian theology results largely from the fact that it is itself a theological casebook. As we grapple with personal needs and decisions in the light of God's presence and purposes, we return to the Bible again and again for motivation, insight, and hope.

MAKING USE OF THE THEOLOGICAL GUIDELINES

The United Methodist emphasis is "practical divinity." How doctrines and beliefs help to shape our experiences and inform our decisions is a matter of critical importance. How our experiences help to shape our theology is of equal concern.

United Methodists seek to *do* theology, not merely to study it. *Doctrinal Standards and Our Theological Task,* therefore, is not a catechism to be memorized. Rather, it is a resource by which United Methodists shape their lives and interpret their experiences. It is also a challenge to continue the task of shaping the faith in the light of personal experience and emerging issues.

Helping persons to think theologically about their personal situations and decisions is an important function of the church. This session seeks to assist persons in doing theology in the midst of their life situations, using the sources and criteria of Scripture, tradition, reason, and experience.

Some rules of thumb for using Scripture, tradition, reason, and experience will help persons who want to think theologically about life situations. Although the four sources and criteria may be discussed as separate entities, they must be seen as a whole and put to use as interrelated and mutually dependent. Each requires the others, and none functions properly without the aid of all.

Using the Bible

Although the authority of Scripture in matters of faith is a basic Christian affirmation, many church members are not familiar with the Bible's stories and message. John Wesley was so steeped in the Bible's language, its images, and its message that Scripture was a natural and inevitable component of his thinking about every issue. That is not the case with many contemporary United Methodists, which means that simply affirming the Bible's centrality or primacy is not enough. Most Christians need help in using the Bible in facing personal issues. Following are a few general guidelines for interpreting Scripture.

First, the Bible is to be read and studied primarily as a book of theology. Although it contains history, science, psychology, and various types of literature, the Bible is principally a book about God and God's relationship to creation and to human beings. It is not meant to be a textbook of science or history. Scripture provides insight into God and God's presence and purpose for life. History is recounted not primarily to provide facts but to reveal God. Facts are less important than the deeper truth of God's presence and purposes.

For example, the Gospel writers do not agree about who reached the empty tomb first, but the *fact* of who arrived first is not the main point of the Resurrection stories. The profound truth beneath the conflicting reports is that the risen Christ has triumphed over sin and death and continues to live and reign.

Second, each part of the Bible is to interpreted in terms of the total message of Scripture. Reading passages in isolation from the broader biblical message results in prooftexting and may distort God's revelation. For example, if considered apart from the main sweep of Scripture, Ecclesiastes would lead one to the conclusion that life has little, if any, ultimate meaning. Read as one part of the total biblical message, Ecclesiastes becomes an important affirmation of the human struggle for meaning.

Third, each book of the Bible must be interpreted first in terms of its historical context. When was it written? Who wrote it? What was the situation the book sought to address? What did it mean to the persons to whom it was written? Before we can know accurately what the Bible *means,* we must know what it *meant.* Severing Scripture from its historical context results in manipulating its message to serve the interpreter's purposes.

Fourth, each passage is to be read and interpreted in its literary context. Where is the passage located? What precedes and follows it in the text? What kind of literature is it? Poetry? Prose? Narrative? Letter? Parable? Allegory? Prophecy? Apocalypse? What literary devices are used? Understanding the literary form and context enables the reader to get inside the biblical material and sense its drama and insight. One can identify with the characters in the stories, experience the surroundings, feel the movements, and confront the issues.

Fifth, after considering the passage in its broader, biblical, historical, and literary contexts, the interpreter begins to raise questions as to the implications for his or her own life and experience: What are the similarities between the situation addressed in the passage and my own situation? What are the differences? What does the passage say about God and God's presence and purposes in and for my life? What difference would it make if I lived in terms of this passage? What changes would take place? What are the hindrances to living in terms of the passage? Does the Bible offer insight and motivation for removing the hindrances?

Using Tradition, Reason, and Experience

United Methodists are likely to be less familiar with church history than they are with the Bible. Although John Wesley was a student of historical theology, few of his heirs in the modern church can readily call upon church tradition as a source and guideline for confronting personal situations and decisions. The historic creeds, however, do provide a concise summary of basic traditional theological parameters. The theological statement itself represents a brief statement of historical theology, and it can be a significant source of help and guidance for persons confronting personal issues of faith.

Except for ethical or theological issues brought on by modern science and theology, few personal issues are new. Persons of faith throughout history have grappled with issues such as sin and guilt, suffering and death, despair and grief, alienation and conflict, war and violence, poverty and injustice, bondage and oppression, sexual expression and exploitation. The search for meaning, the longing for peace, the use and abuse of power, the struggle for political and personal freedom, the seeking to receive and to give love are age-old quests that have received the attention of many of the church's greatest minds. Ignoring the fruit of our ancestors' labors robs us of history's insights and dooms us to repeat its mistakes. Putting our own issues and insights beside those of our forebears for comparison is a responsible means of doing theology.

How can persons who seek God's presence and purpose in their life situations use reason? Obviously, reason is required in order to interpret Scripture and tradition. But reason may also be a channel of new insight and fresh revelation. It is important to recognize that faith and reason are not opposites or antagonists. Reason involves analysis, logic, and reflection and is a faculty given to us by God. Faith, which includes trustful commitment and covenantal relationship, acts on reason and revelation. Faith is commitment in the direction of insights and assumptions, which are reached partly through reason.

Approaching personal situations theologically involves logical analysis of the realities of the circumstances, and it requires that alternatives be explored rationally. Rational evaluation of Scripture and tradition translates the past into the present and enables the person of faith to make maximum use of all sources of revelation.

Reason as a source and criterion, however, can be misleading and deceptive. The intellect can serve selfish ends if not checked against the Bible and tradition. And even when reason is on the right track, it alone will not motivate us. Reason requires that conclusions be verified in experience, one's own and that of others.

Experience, in the Wesleyan tradition, refers to both personal encounter with God's grace and commonsense experience. Personal crises and needs may be experienced as prevenient grace that motivates persons to think theologically about life. Personal experiences also are guidelines by which we validate insights and revelation. God's presence can be known within life's experiences, and life's experiences can be a source and criterion by which persons evaluate affirmations about God.

Experience, like the other sources and criteria, can be misleading. One's personal experience needs the broader experience of others to inform, correct, and support it. Depth psychology reminds us that self-interpretations of experience can be rationalized misrepresentations of reality.

Scripture, tradition, reason, and experience provide persons with resources and guidelines for doing theology in the midst of their life situations. When used as interrelated and mutually dependent tools, they enable persons of faith to deal creatively and wholistically with life's realities and challenges.

A Case Study

John is a thirty-two-year-old husband and father. He and his wife, Karen, have two children, a seven-year-old named Mike and a four-year-old named Ann. John works as a stockbroker and earns approximately seventy-five thousand dollars a year. Karen left her teaching job when the first child was born and has been happy as a homemaker. The family attends church regularly, and their closest friends are church members.

John grew up in a moderately religious family. He largely accepted the beliefs of his church without questioning. He believed that God is all-powerful and that things happen according to a master plan. Although he never stated it in these exact words, he believed that God rewards goodness and punishes evil. John considered himself among the blessed because he enjoyed health, a happy home life, and a profitable and productive job.

One morning while taking a shower John felt a sharp pain when he touched a sore on his back. He didn't think much about it at the time. But when the soreness persisted for a couple of weeks, he decided to check with the doctor. A biopsy was performed, and John was told that the doctor would call when the results were available.

Two days later John received a call from the doctor. "You and Karen need to come down to the office this afternoon," said the doctor. The tone of his voice and the urgency of the appointment warned John of potentially bad news.

Karen and John entered the doctor's office nervously. The doctor entered reading the report and shaking his head slightly. "It's not good news. The biopsy report indicates that you have malignant lymphoma."

"What's that?" John asked hesitantly.

"It's a form of cancer," was the doctor's reply. He proceeded to explain the seriousness of the illness and the proposed treatment with chemotherapy. "It isn't going to be easy, John. But we are going to do everything we can to get you well," commented the doctor.

John checked into the hospital the next day. He would have to remain for at least three weeks in order to receive the chemotherapy.

During the three weeks in the hospital, John became very ill. He didn't feel like seeing anyone. He received lots of cards from friends at church. Many included handwritten notes: "You are in our prayers." "God will bring you through." "Trust God." His pastor visited almost every day. John didn't feel like talking, so the pastor usually would stay a short time and then offer a prayer that God's presence and love would sustain John, Karen, and the children.

Questions began to surface in John's mind about his faith. He prayed for God to heal him and for a sense of peace. Yet his inner turmoil intensified. He assumed that the absence of healing and peace meant God was punishing him. He became increasingly angry and disillusioned.

Finally, John talked with Karen about his feelings of guilt. She suggested that he talk to their pastor the next time he visited. She had joined a Bible study group that meet in the neighborhood. She found support among the women, and they kept assuring her that John would be all right. "You have to have faith, Karen. God can do all things," they told her.

John's pastor entered the room quietly and spoke softly, "How are you feeling today?"

John responded, "Not very well, but I want to talk with you."

The pastor pulled the chair closer to John and said, "Please tell me what's on your mind."

John proceeded to explain his confusion and what he thought of as his lack of faith. "I don't know what I've done to deserve this. I've prayed, and nothing happens. It just doesn't make sense. I'm beginning to wonder even if there is a God. Or if there is, what kind of God would cause or allow something like this? I've always believed God takes care of us if we do what is right. If that is true, then I must have done something wrong. Or maybe God is just a weak God who can't do anything about things like cancer."

The pastor mostly listened. Then he responded, "John, you have raised questions that have baffled some of the best minds in history, so I wouldn't pretend to know the answers. But I would like to explore the questions with you. You're right. It doesn't make sense, and I resist easy answers to your hard questions. Yet you may find comfort in knowing that others, some of whom we consider as being very close to God, have struggled with the same issues. The Bible raises the question over and over again. Job raised it in the Old Testament. He was pretty angry with God. The disciples raised it with Jesus. They asked Jesus if a man's blindness was caused by his sin or by his parents' sin. Jesus refused to accept their assumption that the man's blindness was punishment for sin. Maybe you could reevaluate your assumption that your illness is punishment by God. I would encourage you to read the story of Job, and we will talk about it."

During subsequent visits, John and his pastor discussed the Book of Job and the arguments of Job's friends. John said, "Job seemed to get to the point where he could simply trust God without knowing why he suffered. I'm not there. I'm not sure that's enough for me."

The pastor remarked that acceptance of suffering as mystery and trusting God with it has been one of the traditional answers. He told John that many of the Psalms reflect a longing for that kind of trust, and he encouraged John to use the Psalms as prayers each day. He also suggested that John read Romans 8 and think about it.

Over a period of several weeks, during which John was in and out of the hospital, John and the pastor continued to discuss the issue of suffering. The pastor gave him some books to read, including C. S. Lewis's *The Problem of Pain,* Leslie Weatherhead's *The Will of God,* and Rabbi Harold S. Kushner's *When Bad Things Happen to Good People.* They talked about the various authors' ideas. John said during one of the conversations, "Weatherhead's ideas about the will of God make sense to me. I no longer believe that everything that happens to us is caused directly by God. But it's comforting to feel that nothing that happens to us defeats God's ultimate will. Yet I still have lots of questions. Much of what is happening still doesn't make sense."

The pastor responded, "Yes, and I too have many questions. For me, though, the notion that God causes cancer is incompatible with the God we know in Jesus Christ. The fact that Jesus suffered and died says to me that God under-stands our pain and suffers with us. And did Jesus not cry from the cross, 'My God, my God, why hast thou forsaken me?' "

"I hadn't thought of it that way before," replied John. "Wow, that's mind-boggling! God suffering with me? That sure makes sense. Maybe it's similar to the way we parents suffer with our children, or the way my family and friends have been suffering with me." He was silent for a moment. Then he added, "But God is supposed to be all-powerful."

"That's confusing to me too, John," responded the pastor. "But I have concluded that God's power is the power of love. As I understand the Bible and our tradition, we have two basic assurances. One, God is present with us, even to the close of the age. And, two, God's love for us never ends."

"I'm going to have to think more about this 'power of love.' But I'll have to say that God has been present with me, and I have sensed God's love in all this. You and the family and the church have helped me know and feel that love and presence."

John's Sunday school class was shocked and bewildered by his illness. Class members began asking questions similar to those John raised. The class president talked to the pastor, who suggested that they might want to spend some time as a group studying and discussing the problem of suffering. He suggested that they begin with a consideration of what the Bible says and then look at what some of the great teachers of the church wrote on the matter.

The pastor volunteered to teach the class for three months. During these sessions, participants discussed the ideas presented by the pastor in light of their own experience and understanding. Although John was unable to attend Sunday school, his situation was always on their minds. His wife attended the class several Sundays, and her presence always brought a sense of reality to the study.

Conclusion

John's illness was accompanied by a crisis of faith. Beliefs previously held were called into question by John, his family, his friends, and his pastor. They all participated in the theological task created by John's situation. John's experience of suffering resulted in their reevaluating Scripture, tradition, and reason. They used the four sources and guidelines for doing theology effectively in responding to the crisis of faith.

The pastor acknowledged the primacy of Scripture as both a source and criterion by pointing to the Book of Job, the Psalms, and Romans. Reading and discussing the Bible's approaches to the reality of suffering gave John permission to raise questions and provided various options for understanding suffering. The assurance that John's questions had been raised by some of history's brightest and best persons helped to relieve his guilt for raising them and provided a sense of hope for some resolution to his questions.

Both Scripture and tradition were for John sources of new insights and criteria by which he evaluated his own experience and reason. Yet he also criticized Scripture and tradition in terms of his own reason and experience. Job's affirmation of trust in the face of suffering, for example, was helpful; but John admitted that he had yet to reach that level of trust in his own experience. He further acknowledged that he still had many unanswered questions. The theological task remained unfinished.

The decision of the Sunday school class to study and discuss the issue of suffering grew out of John's experience, and John's experience kept the study from being merely an intellectual consideration of concepts and theories. In other words, "practical divinity" was the goal.

A final word regarding the response to John's illness and crisis of faith merits consideration. As the community of faith (the church), engaged in the theological task, God's love and presence became incarnate, John's *experience* of God's grace came in relationship with the pastor, his family, and friends and through his interaction with Scripture and tradition. The theological task, indeed, belongs to the whole church; and it is in doing theology in the face of personal and societal issues and decisions that the church is the church.

THE SESSION PLAN

1. Make or have members of the class make before the session a mobile of the four sources and criteria—Scripture, tradition, reason, and experience. Arrange the four parts of the mobile to indicate the centrality of Scripture. Place *Scripture* in the middle, on a large piece of posterboard and in a brighter color. Have *Tradition, Reason,* and *Experience* rotate around *Scripture.* Hang the mobile in a prominent location in the room, where it can be seen by all class members.

Begin the session by reviewing the four guidelines as both sources and criteria for theology. Point out that Scripture is central and that all are interrelated and mutually dependent.

An alternative way of beginning is to have the parts for the mobile available (posterboard cards for the sources and criteria, string, and clothes hanger). Point to Scripture, tradition, reason, and experience as sources and criteria. Then ask the class members to help assemble and hang the pieces.

2. Remind class members of these important points: (1) The Wesleyan emphasis is on "practical divinity." Therefore, we are concerned about theology and its relationship to real-life situations. (2) The theological task remains unfinished as we interpret the Christian faith in light of our own experiences and needs. (3) Theology belongs to the whole church, not just to professional theologians and pastors. (4) We all *do* theology, whether or not we call it theology, as we consider beliefs about God and experiences of God in the light of personal situations and decisions.

3. The sources and criteria are not new with Wesley. They can be seen in biblical portrayals of persons facing personal situations demanding decisions. Have class members read the story of Zacchaeus in Luke 19:1-10, looking for the roles of Scripture, tradition, reason, and experience in the story. Discuss the findings either as a total class or in teams. Refer to the comments in the leader's guide as needed to guide the discussion.

4. Either read to the class or have copies distributed of John's story. Have class members answer the following questions:

What role did experience play? (Caused a crisis of faith and motivated inquiry, evaluated Scripture and tradition, became a vehicle of grace as John experienced love from others.)

How was tradition used? (Provided assurance and support for raising questions, gave insight and raised new questions, gave a sense of continuity with others who had suffered and questioned their faith.)

What role did reason serve? (It was a means by which John raised questions, evaluated possible answers, and integrated the insights he gained.)

What impact did John's experience have on his Sunday school class? in what ways did the members of the class fulfill their ministry in accordance with the statement in the *Discipline* of the ministry of all Christians? (*Discipline,* ¶¶ 126–129; student book, pages 57–58).

5. Present the following situation or another one like it that you create or find elsewhere:

Susan is a forty-eight-year-old engineer who has recently gone through a divorce after being married for twenty-two years. She and her ex-husband had no children. She went to a Methodist church with her mother and father until she was a junior in high school. She attended her first worship service in more than thirty years just two weeks ago.

The church Susan attended sends a layperson to call on each visitor to the church. When someone came to call on her, Susan welcomed the visitor. After a few minutes of pleasant conversation, she said, "I'm not sure I'm interested in the church. I went because I'm lonely and thought it might be a place to make friends, but I have some real problems with the church. I can't believe all those doctrines, so I'm not a Christian. I remember when I was in the fourth grade I had some doubts about the world being created in six days. I asked my mother if I had to believe everything the Bible says and the church teaches in order to go to heaven. She said I had to believe the Bible and just accept it on faith. Well, I can't do that. You see, I believe in evolution and I just can't accept many of the Bible stories."

She went on to say that she considered herself a "good person who loves people." She specifically asked about the church's programs to help the poor. Finally Susan said, "I appreciate your coming. I'll have to admit that something is stirring inside me, and for some reason I felt the need to go to church. But I don't want to be a hypocrite and pretend that I believe things that I don't believe. I've got a lot of doubts and questions, so I probably don't fit into the church. How does your church deal with people like me?"

6. Divide the class into four teams that will respond to Susan's question and situation. Assign one team to represent Scripture, another tradition, another reason, and another experience. Have each team prepare a response to Susan's situation from its assigned perspective. Allow twenty to thirty minutes for the groups to work.

If your church has a library, encourage team members to consult the library. If possible, have available in the classroom resources such as Bibles, concordances, dictionaries, and commentaries, *The Westminster Dictionary of Christian Theology*, writings of Luther, Calvin, Augustine, Wesley, and perhaps a few more contemporary writers such as Georgia Harkness, Leslie Weatherhead's *The Christian Agnostic*, Harry Emerson Fosdick's *Dear Mr. Brown*, Frederick Buechner's *Alphabet of Grace*, John Cobb's *On Becoming a Thinking Christian*, or other books you have found helpful in dealing with doubt and faith. The chapter by Roger E. Timm in *Cosmos as Creation: Theology and Science in Consonance*, edited by Ted Peters, provides a good summary of the controversy about evolution and the biblical notion of creation.

7. After allowing time for work in teams, reconvene the class and ask each team to present in some way its response to Susan's situation. How does Scripture respond? Tradition? Reason? Experience? One likely result is the awareness that the issues cannot be dealt with by the sources and criteria in isolation from one another. Tradition will have called upon Scripture and Scripture upon tradition, and

reason and experience will interact with Scripture and tradition.

Do not be surprised if groups feel frustrated by lack of time and adequate resources. The exercise should illustrate our need for more understanding of Scripture and tradition, and it will demonstrate the limitations of our experience and reason. Make the point that the criteria and sources are to be used within the context of community. Individuals apart from the support and correction of the community often misinterpret Scripture, fragment tradition, pervert experience, and twist reason. We need each other as we do theology!

8. Ask class members to write on a card or sheet of paper their responses to this question: What situations or decisions do I currently face that call for additional theological reflection and inquiry?

After allowing persons time to write their responses, invite them to report to the class. Some issues may be too personal for class members to feel comfortable sharing publicly. You might invite them to leave the responses with you, either signed or unsigned. The responses will likely reveal areas for fruitful study groups within the church. Perhaps persons who have similar issues can get together for discussion of them, using the criteria of Scripture, tradition, reason, and experience.

9. Close the session with the following prayer or another of your choice:

"O God, who meets us within life's joys and pains, its hope and despair, its victories and defeats, its answers, and its questions: We are thankful for resources that enable us to know your presence and purposes, for Scripture that bears witness to your eternal Word, for tradition that transmits the truth and insights of the past, for reason that analyzes and appropriates your revelation, and for experience that incarnates your truth. We praise you, O God. Through your prodding and redeeming presence, lead us in the unending journey toward the fulfillment of your purposes for us and all creation; through Jesus Christ our Lord. Amen."

A CHANGING WORLD
AND THE CHURCH'S MISSION AND MINISTRY

Purpose of This Session:

To help adults identify some of the critical current developments in our society and in the world that call for renewal, imaginative theological reflection, and renewed commitment to the church's mission and ministry.

Goals of This Session:

1. To challenge adults to participate in the continuing theological task as part of the church's mission.
2. To help adults identify several critical issues that merit theological reflection and leadership by the church.
3. To enable adults to see how our United Methodist heritage contributes to the ongoing process of theological reflection and missional involvement.

GROUNDING IN SCRIPTURE

Scripture reveals the unfinished nature of the theological task and the ongoing mission of the people of God. The Bible itself reflects the continuous revelation of God, who cannot be defined by a single name (Exodus 3:13-14), limited to a prescribed place (1 Kings 8:27; Ezekiel 1; Acts 7:47-50), or contained in any symbols (Acts 19:26). God is known and experienced in the unfolding of history; and the Bible reflects the unfolding nature of God's revelation and persistent mission to heal, redeem, and transform all creation into the reign of God.

The various books of the Bible reflect the ongoing task of discerning and sharing in the activity and purposes of God. Each book was written in response to specific historical situations that call for theological reflection and

faithful ministry by the covenant community. For example, the eighth-century prophetic writings of Amos, Hosea, Micah, and Isaiah represent the prophets' inspired perception of the implications of the approaching destruction of the nations of Israel and Judah. What did the rising threat of Assyria and the moral and political decline of Israel and Judah say about God and God's relationship to Israel? Where had these nations failed to fulfill their covenant with God? What did the existence of poverty, violence, and national collapse have to say about God and the people whom God had called to be "a light to the nations"? These were among the unfinished theological missional tasks of eighth-century Palestine.

The Four Gospels represent the growing understanding in the early church of God's revelation in Jesus Christ. Each Gospel is an interpretation of the whole Christ event in light of particular emerging needs of the early church as it confronted new situations and different cultures. How was the gospel to be interpreted and lived in Hellenistic culture? What does it mean to be faithful to Jesus Christ in a hostile political and cultural environment?

Other New Testament writings are examples of the ongoing theological task as persons of faith sought to live out their faith in the context of personal and community issues. The Book of Revelation, for example, confronts the issue of God's sovereignty and the fulfillment of God's purposes during a time when Roman power seemed to be sovereign and God's purposes were being defeated by persecution and idolatry.

Scripture reveals a God whose nature and purposes become known as persons and com-

90

munities of faith seek to understand and live by their faith. The writers sought to discern the will of God by remembering God's previous revelation, through personal and communal worship and prayer, and by obeying the will of God. They assumed that new situations require new insights and new strategies for being agents of God's healing, redeeming, and transforming grace.

Contemporary personal and global realities require that the ancient truths of Scripture be interpreted in light of emerging issues and applied to those issues; and, they require that the church clarify its mission and ministry as it confronts the crises of the present age. Several key biblical affirmations particularly demand continuing theological reflection in the context of current realities.

First, according to the Bible, creation has its origin and purpose in God (Genesis 1–2; Psalm 24; Isaiah 42:5-6). All of creation belongs to God, and human beings are an integral and important part of creation. Humans are given the responsibility to care for creation (Genesis 1:26; 2:15; Psalm 8:6-8). What God has created is good, and human beings are accountable to God for the use of creation's resources.

Second, God hears the cries of the poor, delivers the oppressed, defends the widows and the orphans and the immigrants, identifies with the impoverished and most vulnerable (Exodus 3:7-11; Deuteronomy 10:12-20; Psalms 46:4-6 and 146; Isaiah 1:12-17; Luke 2:52-55 and 4:16-19; Matthew 25:31-46; 1 Corinthians 1:18-26). The church is to imitate this God (Ephesians 5:1-2), and the people of God are to be judged on the basis of their response to the suffering, vulnerable, impoverished, and marginalized (Matthew 25:31-46). Ministry is participation with the suffering and vulnerable God who in Jesus Christ comes as One who is poor, homeless, despised, and crucified. Sharing in Christ's ministry, then, is a call to servanthood (Exodus 3:7ff.; Isaiah 53; Mark 8:31-38; Matthew 25:31-46; Philippians 2:1-11).

Third, Scripture affirms the oneness of the human family under the sovereignty of God (Amos 9:7-8; Jonah; Acts 10:34-35; 17:26; Ephesians 2:14-16). God, from the dawn of cre-ation, has sought to reconcile the world and its people to the divine purpose. Peace, justice, and goodwill among people and nations are the goals toward which God is seeking to move the world. Human beings play a crucial role in the fulfillment of God's vision of *shalom* and the coming of God's reign. Justice for the poor, the weak, and the needy is a major demand that God places on the human family (Isaiah 61:1-2; Amos 5:21-24; Micah 6:8; Matthew 25:31-46; James 1:29–2:9).

Fourth, the Bible affirms the existence of a personal God who works in the natural world and in history. This God became incarnate in Jesus Christ, who was fully human and fully divine and in whose sacrificial death and resurrection triumphed over sin and death. In Christ God has reconciled the human family, and through the Holy Spirit God sustains and guides human beings toward their ultimate fulfillment. Such biblical affirmations, timeless in their truth, require reinterpretation and application in a world dominated by exploding scientific knowledge and widespread trust in and reliance upon technology.

Scripture itself reflects the unfinished and ongoing nature of the theological task and the church's mission. Scripture also provides foundational insights and affirmations by which continuing theological work and ministry are done. So the contemporary church continues to grapple with emerging needs and realities in the light of God's revelation in Scripture and God's continuing self-disclosure in history, experience, and reason.

WHAT THE *DISCIPLINE* SAYS
(*Discipline*, ¶ 104, and Parts III and V; student book, pages 42–64)

"In addition to historic tensions and conflicts that still require resolution, new issues continually arise that summon us to fresh theological inquiry" (*Discipline*, ¶ 104; student book, page 51). United Methodists affirm that the efforts to understand and apply the truth and reality of God are never completed. God's nature, purposes, and activity transcend all doctrinal formulations, all historic contexts, and all institutional strategies. Yet God is known and God's will is done in specific historical contexts. Discerning God's will and participating in God's reign require continuing theological reflection and missional commitment by the people of God.

Religious truth must always be evaluated in the light of new insights and additional revelations; otherwise, past formulations and images become idols to a static deity rather than footsteps of a dynamic God who is making all things new. Discoveries in science and emerging global realities make it necessary for the church to reapply ancient truths, and they challenge the church to proclaim the timeless message in new images. These realities confronting the world call the church to evaluate its ministry and seek new ways to be a sign and herald of God's vision for the world.

The following represent some of the particular challenges confronting the church. This is not an exhaustive list but an invitation to United Methodists to engage seriously in the unfinished theological task and to share in God's ministry to the world through the church.

The World as a Global Village, Filled With Diversity and Suffering

A global community with diverse values, ideologies, political systems, and with limited resources presents new challenges for the church. Modern means of communication and transportation have brought peoples of the world closer together. Economic realities have intensified interdependency among nations so that the stock market on one side of the world radically influences the market on the other side of the world. Muslims, Hindus, Jews, and Christians no longer live in homogeneous communities isolated from one another. Competing political and economic systems confront one another in the arena of world opinion.

The global village of diverse people, ideologies, and systems is armed with weapons powerful enough to alter life radically or perhaps to destroy it altogether. Pollution and depletion threaten limited natural resources. Economic disparity, violence, and needless suffering threaten the abundant life that God seeks for all people.

An estimated forty million people die of poverty-related causes each year. More than forty thousand children under the age of five perish from malnutrition every day. Science and technology have made available the technical resources to produce enough food to feed the world's hungry; and medical cures are available to prevent most fatal childhood diseases. Yet, more people die needlessly from hunger and disease than ever before.

In such a village, what do the biblical and historical doctrines of creation and stewardship mean? How are God's people to respond to global environmental realities and the availability of resources? What does it mean to cultivate and care for creation? What responsibility do affluent Christians have toward the world's poor? What are the implications for the church in the United States if the God we are to imitate is One who identifies with the poor, the vulnerable, and the suffering? Is this the God that is shaping our churches?

The *Discipline* affirms "servant ministry and servant leadership," stating, "The ministry of all Christians consists of service for the mission of God in the world" (¶ 131; student book, pages 58–59). What does servanthood mean in the midst of the adverse and widespread poverty in the world? What does servanthood mean for the individual disciple of Jesus? The local congregation? The ordained clergy, deacons, and elders? Struggling with such questions requires considerable theological reflection in the light of Scripture, tradition, experience, and reason.

The Bible affirms the oneness of the human family under the sovereignty of God. Yet the religions of the world have varying understandings of God, and they often contribute to divisions and hostility within the global village. If God is active in the history of all people and Christ is sovereign over all (Colossians 1:15-20), what is to be our relationship with other religions? How are we to fulfill the mission of the church to make disciples of Jesus Christ when other religions claim a different means of salvation? What does "the oneness of the human family" mean in the context of racial, political, theological, and socioeconomic diversity? How can the church be a "counter-community" and live out the oneness of the human family in response to God's sovereignty?

God's vision for the world includes peace:
"He [God] shall judge between the nations,
and shall arbitrate for many peoples;
they shall beat their swords into plowshares,
and their spears into pruning hooks;
nation shall not lift up sword against nation,
neither shall they learn war any more"
(Isaiah 2:4).

Yet in the global village, nations continue to build more and more weapons of destruction. The contemporary image of the world as a global village, populated with diverse peoples with varying ideologies and socioeconomic and political systems, presents pressing theological questions to the church. What is to be the nature and mission of the church in a global village? What should be its priorities, and how is its common life to be ordered? What does it mean to be a minister of Jesus Christ in such a world?

Science and Technology

A second contemporary reality that presents the challenge of further theological reflection to the church is modern science and technology. The so-called scientific revolution has changed the way people view creation itself. People look to science and technology for solutions to basic problems and as primary explanations of the origin and function of the natural order. How is God as Creator to be understood in light of scientific explanations of the origin of life? How are we to make the pre-scientific images and symbols of the Bible meaningful to modern minds more familiar with biology, physics, chemistry, and computers than with theology, doctrine, and the Bible?

Many modern scientists on the cutting edge of science have rediscovered a sense of the mystery and dynamic nature of the universe. During the nineteenth century and the first part of the twentieth century, the word *mystery* was seldom, if ever, used in scientific writings because it was widely believed that science was rapidly dispelling all mysteries. Now there seems to be a recovery of mystery.

After serving as the pastor of many scientists in Oak Ridge, Tennessee, I am convinced that modern scientists are among the church's most important potential allies and among its most diligent theological inquirers. Many contemporary scientists stand in awe, reverence, and humility before the mystery of the universe—a stance more in keeping with the biblical view than that of many of the dogmatic pronouncements of some pastors and religious leaders.

How can religion and science join in a cooperative expedition into the mysteries of life? What insights does theology offer to science? What insights does science offer to theology?

Developments in science and technology raise critical theological and ethical issues. For example, biology confirms that up to 97 percent of the molecules that make up the human body are the same as those in other forms of biological life. What are the implications of that fact for our understanding of the uniqueness of human beings and the relationship between human beings and the rest of creation? Are human beings predominantly *participants* in creation or *dominators* of creation? Geneticists are discovering that many characteristics, traits, and predispositions to illnesses and diseases are determined genetically. What is the impact of such data upon the biblical and traditional concepts of free will, sin, and salvation?

Most issues faced by scientists and technologists have to do with values and ethics. The ability to create, alter, prolong, and terminate life creates complex ethical dilemmas for the whole society, and the church must have a voice in the debates. What should be the nature and content of that voice? The future direction of scientific research and technology is a legitimate concern of the theological community. Shall science and technology be propelled by profits? By national security? By service to the common good? Who should make the decisions about what research to do and which technology to develop?

**Vastness of Space
and Impersonal Modern Life**

Another reality that challenges the church to continued theological inquiry and faithful ministry is the new awareness of the vastness of space and the impersonal nature of modern life. Given the endless expanse of space and the innumerable species of life, the ancient question of the psalmist has increased modern relevance:

"When I look at your heavens,
        the work of your fingers,
        the moon and the stars that
        you have established;
    what are human beings that you
        are mindful of them,
        mortals that you care for them?"
            (Psalm 8:3-4).

The traditional belief in a personal God who loves and cares for individuals must be communicated in fresh images and relevant experiences. Otherwise, belief in God will be relegated to a narrow compartment of life and rendered irrelevant.

Belief in God is not necessarily a virtue. The kind of God we believe in and our relationship with God make all the difference. Many persons affirm the existence of God in the same manner that they affirm the existence of distant galaxies. They assume that the galaxies exist but know nothing of the galaxies' natures and locations. They have no relationship with the galaxies and only speculate about them. Belief in the existence of God has no influence on their daily lives.

The biblical image of a God who knows our names and is present with and cares about every aspect of creation is threatened by a mechanistic, impersonal view of life. How are persons to know and experience the presence and love of God? What do we mean by *God*? Is God to be thought of in terms of *a* being itself? Is God more like an impersonal power such as electricity, which we can experience only in terms of its results? Or is God more like a parent or friend whom we can know and love? What experiences may we identify as the presence of God? Does God violate natural laws and perform miracles? How does God work in the world?

The impersonal nature of modern living presents the church with abundant opportunities for ministry through personal relationships and servanthood. As a covenant community in which people are held in love and held accountable, the church must resist an institutionalism that contributes to depersonalizing of others. Is there a conflict between the church as a social institution with many members, multiple activities, and complex structures and the church as a caring community shaped by a personal God who knows and cares about even the most unnoticed person? What is the role of ordained ministers in an impersonal world?

The world as a global village filled with diverse and suffering people, modern science and technology, and the vastness of space and impersonal nature of modern life are only three of the contemporary challenges to the church. They challenge the church to continued exploration into the mystery of God's presence, purposes, and power. The challenges may be invitations from the One who said, "When you search for me, you will find me; if you seek me with all your heart, I will let you find me" (Jeremiah 29:13-14). It is precisely in such a world that God is found and served.

RESOURCES FOR THE UNFINISHED TASK

United Methodism provides exceptional resources with which to face contemporary theological challenges. Our heritage is one of intellectual honesty, freedom of inquiry, and missional zeal. Commitment to loving God with the mind and a concern for "practical divinity" compel United Methodists to approach the ongoing task with humility and openness and a willingness to move into new avenues of ministry and mission.

Doctrinal Emphases

One resource with which United Methodists meet the new demands and challenges is a core of doctrine that provides stability amid change. The distinctive doctrinal emphases of the Wesleyan heritage provide for flexibility as well as stability. Both are necessary for creative and responsible theological exploration. Without flexibility, theological inquiry is nothing more than reactionary defensiveness. Without stability, however, theological inquiry is subject to faddish relativism and rigid rationalism.

Part of the core of United Methodist doctrine is belief in the triune God, who is present in all of life and invites us to share in the divine life and mission. The trinitarian concept of God provides a framework for understanding God in new and diverse images while maintaining a firm belief in a personal God. The doctrine of the Trinity affirms God's revelation of the divine reality and presence in creation, in Jesus Christ, and in the Holy Spirit. It also affirms that no formulation or image can fully describe God; therefore, United Methodists can face the current challenges to our understanding of God with openness to new insights while being anchored in belief in God. Since community is part of the nature of God, we can take seriously the diversity in the human family and see it as an intimation of the Eternal One.

Another doctrinal resource is the distinctive emphasis on salvation by grace. The language may require interpretation and alteration, but the reality of grace remains relevant in any age. The experience of self-worth rooted in whom we belong rather than in what we know, what we have, or what we can do provides security amid change. Grace also affirms the worth and dignity of all people; therefore, we must reach out in friendship, service, and justice to those most vulnerable. Since God has claimed the least, the poor, the marginalized, as recipients and means of grace, ministry involves receiving the gifts of those with whom God is present in special ways. Approaching life as a gift from a gracious and loving God who is always working on behalf of the human family enables us to face new theological and missional challenges with hope and assurance.

Furthermore, the summons to "holy living," "scriptural holiness," "perfection in love," and "practical divinity" as response to grace still calls forth the highest possible ethical life. Science and technology have placed before us new dimensions of holy living. What does holiness mean in the context of such issues as abortion, ecological threats, power politics, and economic disparity? United Methodists have a tradition of coping with such ambiguity while holding fast to the goal of reforming the nation and spreading scriptural holiness throughout the land.

Finally, United Methodism's ecumenical approach and "catholic spirit" enable us to face the continuing theological and missional task as partners with other denominations and other faiths. Our understanding of the whole church as the body of Christ avoids sectarianism and denominational arrogance. United Methodists make no claim of superiority in the pursuit of God's unfolding truth and purposes. We are open to dialogue and partnership with others involved in the unfinished theological and missional task.

Theological Guidelines

United Methodists face the ongoing theological and missional task with the resource of a core of doctrine and with four guidelines for theological exploration, as seen in Session 9.

Although many of the specific issues that challenge contemporary theology have no specific reference in Scripture, Scripture provides sound ethical and moral principles for Christians in considering current issues. The Bible remains the central source for exploration into God's will and purpose for the modern world.

Tradition enables United Methodists to avoid forgetting the past and the ancient, timeless truths. Theology and ministry do not start over in a new era. Instead, we use the resources of history as means of understanding the present and the future and effectively fulfilling our servant ministry. The challenges that the church faces have historical antecedents. Subjecting emerging issues to the test of tradition is part of the task of theology.

Issues the church confronts require the application of reason. Jesus' advice to the disciples who were launching into new avenues of ministry and witness has never been more relevant than it is in the modern world: "Be wise as serpents and innocent as doves" (Matthew 10:16).

The fourth guideline or resource for the ongoing theological and missional task is experience. When the criterion of experience is applied to current challenges, theology remains practical and relevant. Current challenges may also be a means of expanding and deepening our experience of God as we meet the risen Christ in the midst of the struggles to be faithful disciples.

Conclusion

The task of exploring the nature, purposes, and activity of God remains fresh and demanding in every age. Since God is more than is known or experienced, and since the world is not yet the kingdom of God, the theological and missional task remains unfinished.

The world as a global village of diverse people with varying ideologies and systems presents significant theological challenges to the church. Modern science and technology require additional exploration into the nature and activity of God, and they present the church with significant moral and ethical dilemmas and abundant opportunities to be in ministry. The vastness of space and the impersonal nature of modern life raise questions regarding the significance and uniqueness of human beings and their relationship to God. The mission of the church to make disciples of Jesus Christ has become all the more urgent.

The church continues theological inquiry with the resources of foundational doctrines and with proven guidelines. We confront the present challenges with the timeless truth of Scripture, the insights of tradition, the resources of reason, and the sensitivities of experience. Firm grounding in our Wesleyan heritage and in our current doctrinal position enables us to continue the unfinished task with adventure, servanthood, joy, and hope.

THE SESSION PLAN

1. Begin the session by passing around a sheet of paper on which is written, "God is . . ." and "God's purpose for the world includes. . . ." Ask each group member to write a word or sentence that describes God and God's dream for the world. Then pass the sheet on to the next person. After all group members have written one or more descriptive words or sentences, ask these questions: Does this list totally describe God and God's purpose for the world? (The description of God and God's activity is always unfinished and incomplete.) Why? (Because God transcends all description; God's activity is dynamic rather than static; and, God's kingdom is both a present reality and a future hope.)

2. In order to demonstrate that the Bible itself shows the ongoing nature of the theological task, select a theme and trace its development in the Bible. You may choose any one of a number of concepts, including the understanding of God, of life after death, of the treatment of enemies, or of the meaning and use of wealth. The emergence of the idea of monotheism, belief in one God, is rehearsed here for your convenience.

The early Hebrews believed in the existence of many gods, but Yahweh was considered to be the chief or dominant God (Exodus 15:11; 34:14; Deuteronomy 6:14). Gradually, Yahweh came to be seen as the only God (Isaiah 45:22; 46:9). God was first viewed as dwelling primarily on the holy mountain (Exodus 19:3-6), then in the Holy City of Jerusalem and the Temple (2 Samuel 22:7; Ezra 1:3-5). God finally came to be seen as being everywhere (Psalm 139:7-10; Acts 17:27-28). God is to be worshiped as Spirit (John 4:24) and cannot be confined to temples made with hands (Acts 7:48; 17:24).

Have class members look up the Scripture references in the order above. Ask them to read aloud the passages' descriptions of God. As they read these descriptions, point out that the understanding of God grew throughout the Bible, reaching its fullest revelation in Jesus Christ.

Other aspects of God's nature and activity can be traced similarly by using a dictionary of the Bible or a theological word book. A review of God's relationship to the poor and oppressed would be an especially useful exercise.

3. Briefly mention that the view of the universe in the Bible and in much of the church's history predates discoveries in astronomy, biology, chemistry, and physics. For example, ancient people believed in a three-storied universe. A flat earth, with a dome-shaped sky overhead, was at the center; above the sky was water; and, beneath the earth was Sheol. The sun and moon were seen as rotating around the earth. We now know that space is infinite; there is no dome overhead. The earth rotates around the sun and is not the center of the universe.

Explain that a change in worldview has brought about changes in how we envision and talk about God. One twentieth-century theologian, Dietrich Bonhoeffer, contends that we must no longer consider God as "the God of the gaps." People, according to Bonhoeffer, have tended to use God to fill in the gaps of their knowledge. They attributed to God phenomena or events that they didn't understand. As knowledge of the universe increases, God has been removed from it. Bonhoeffer challenges the church to rethink its image of God and to recover a sense of the deeper meaning of mystery.

Other theologians are challenging us to broaden our concept of God. J. B. Phillips's little book *Your God Is Too Small* is a helpful resource for laypersons. It would be helpful to have a class member read it and provide a brief report to the class.

4. Arrange a panel consisting of an astronomer, a physicist, a biologist, a chemist, and your pastor. If no scientists are available, perhaps one or two high school science teachers can be invited. Ask them to respond to these questions: What major changes have come about in the understanding of the universe during the last three hundred years? What are some of the implications of these changes for religion? What current key developments in science represent a challenge to religion? In what ways do you see science and religion working together?

OR

4. Review the section of this leader's guide on realities in the contemporary world that represent challenges to the church (the world as a global village made up of diverse peoples, ideologies, and systems; the vastness of space and the impersonal nature of modern life; confidence in science and technology as sources of explanations of life's meaning and as solutions to life's problems).

5. Read aloud the following quotation from Dr. William Pollard, a physicist and Episcopal priest: "It is possible to present all fields of knowledge—science, philosophy, history, psychology, sociology, and literature—without sacrifice of critical judgment, objectivity, or complete honesty in such a way that all that we are and all that we know fits together again into the Christian rather than the secular view of existence. This task is the special assignment of the Christian Church today. It is a crucial, terribly important task in these cruel days."[1]

Ask these questions: Do you agree with Dr. Pollard's contention that all knowledge can fit into the Christian view of existence? If so, where do you see current conflicts in understanding between the scientific view and the Christian view of existence? (People may list many conflicts: creation and evolution, natural law and miracles, the biological similarity of humans and other animals and the biblical view of humans as being "little less than God," the emerging information about genetic determination and human freedom of the will, medical science's ability to create life in a test tube and prolong life by mechanical means and the theological affirmation of God as the source of life's beginning and ending.)

Then ask this question: How can we as individuals and as a church deal with these issues? Solicit suggestions from the total group and write them on chalkboard or a sheet of paper. Possible suggestions may include: (1) learning more about the Bible and our beliefs so that we can be clearer about what is the "Christian view of existence"; (2) sponsoring special seminars and studies on the issues; (3) promoting dialogue between scientists and religious leaders by bringing them together to talk about issues such as creation and environmental concerns, world peace and nuclear weapons, the sacredness of life and abortion; ethical issues involved in genetic engineering; (4) participating in a Volunteer in Mission project or inviting persons who work with the impoverished, the imprisoned, and so on, to share why they are involved and what such involvement teaches them about God.

6. Invite two clergy, preferably one deacon and one elder (as described in *Discipline*, ¶ 137; student book, pages 60–61), and two laypersons to

form a panel to discuss their understanding of the ministry of all Christians and how they fulfill their ministry of servanthood and servant leadership. Ask them to comment on the implications of the church realities described in the leader's guide on how they perceive and practice ministry. Ask the class to be aware of the ways that doctrine and the guidelines and sources for theological reflection influence the persons' approach to ministry.

7. The United Methodist Church provides two basic resources with which to approach the ongoing task of knowing God and discerning God's will: (1) a core of doctrine or beliefs and (2) guidelines for theological inquiry. Write "Doctrines" and "Guidelines" on chalkboard or posterboard as headings of two vertical columns. On the basis of previous sessions, what would you list as the core doctrines that provide a foundation for considering contemporary issues? List doctrines as class members suggest them. If they need reminders, have them look back through the theological statement.

After doctrines have been listed, ask participants to name the United Methodist guidelines—Scripture, tradition, reason, experience. List them under "Guidelines."

8. If time permits, choose one of the issues (such as creation and evolution) and begin to discuss it on the basis of the doctrinal resources and the guidelines listed in Activity 7. Use these questions: Do the core doctrines conflict with evolution? What insights can be gained from Scripture? Tradition? Reason? Experience?

9. Close with this prayer for the church:

"O God our Father, we pray for thy Church, which is set today amid the perplexities of a changing order, and face to face with new tasks. Baptize her afresh in the life-giving spirit of Jesus! Bestow upon her a great responsiveness to duty, a swifter compassion with suffering, and an utter loyalty to the will of God. Help her to proclaim boldly the coming of the kingdom of God. Put upon her lips the ancient Gospel of her Lord. Fill her with the prophets' scorn of tyranny, and with a Christ-like tenderness for the heavy-laden and downtrodden. Bid her cease from seeking her own life, lest she lose it. Make her valiant to give up her life to humanity, that, like her crucified Lord, she may mount by the path of the cross to a higher glory; through the same Jesus Christ our Lord. Amen."[2]

OR

9. Close by singing or reciting the hymn "God of Grace and God of Glory" (*The United Methodist Hymnal*, Number 577).

---

[1] From *Transcendence and Providence*, by William G. Pollard (Scottish Academic Press, 1987), page 25.

[2] From *The Book of Worship.* Copyright © 1964, 1965 by Board of Publication of The Methodist Church, Inc., page 184.

Session 12

NEW THEOLOGICAL EXPLORATIONS

Purpose of This Session:
To help adults become aware of some of the recent developments in theology that have emerged as responses to the challenges of our world.

Goals of This Session:
1. To help adults see that theology grows out of specific historical and cultural situations.
2. To introduce adults to some contemporary developments in theology.
3. To allow participants to practice using the insights of some recent theological developments in dealing with personal and societal issues.

GROUNDING IN SCRIPTURE

God's revelation comes within specific historical and personal experiences. God's truth emerges as persons and communities of faith struggle to understand the realities of their world in the light of God's nature and purposes. Theology evaluates current experiences and realities by the criteria of God's presence and purpose, and theology is reinterpreted by current realities and experiences.

The Bible reflects the dynamic and diverse nature of theology. Although it holds firmly to certain basic affirmations. Scripture engages in theological exploration as new situations are encountered. The basic affirmation of God's covenant with Israel, for example, had to be reinterpreted when the nation faced destruction and exile. The writings of Amos, Hosea, Micah, Isaiah, Jeremiah, Ezekiel, and others represent theological inquiry and exploration in the context of national collapse and injustice.

The prophet Habakkuk reflected on the implication of the belief that God was using the Babylonians to punish Judah for its sins. Other prophets had proclaimed that the impending national destruction resulted from Judah's failure to practice justice, righteousness, faithfulness, and obedience to God. To Habakkuk, it seems curious that God would use a less righteous nation to destroy Judah, which was more faithful, just, and righteous than Babylonia. He apparently reflected and built on the theology of prophets such as Isaiah.

Perhaps the most obvious example in the New Testament of theological inquiry growing out of the life situations of the people of faith is the Book of Revelation. The Roman emperor Domitian attempted to force emperor worship on Christians. His reign was a period of cruel persecution of the faithful. To a people who expected the imminent return of Christ, who would conquer all foes and establish the reign of God, the cruel domination of Rome was a crisis of faith. Many faced martyrdom. The temptation to renounce the faith was strong. Despair, hopelessness, and disillusionment threatened the church's future.

In the context of persecution and hopelessness, apocalyptic writings emerged. Revelation poetically and imaginatively proclaims a message of hope and judgment. Apocalyptic emphases differ from those of the prophetic writings. The view of God and how God works in history varies somewhat between apocalyptic and prophetic literature. This difference illustrates that theology emerges from and reflects life situations. The two kinds of writing have the same basic images and concepts.

Scripture provides a foundation for continuing theological inquiry in light of emerging realities and issues. And current developments in theology are rooted in Scripture. As persons of faith confront realities of the modern world, the Bible becomes a source of insight and a criterion for evaluating ongoing theological exploration.

Process theology, for instance, finds roots in the biblical doctrine of Creation. Genesis 1 describes God's creative activity as bringing order out of chaos. The interdependency of all creation is affirmed, and God's power is manifested in the ongoing movement of the created order toward unity amid diversity.

Liberation theology places emphasis on God's liberating activity in overcoming all forms of oppression and bondage. The Exodus proclaims God's goal of conquering slavery and oppression. The prophetic tradition and Jesus' ministry proclaim God's opposition to injustice, exploitation, and bondage. God champions the cause of the poor and those who lack access to political and economic power. Jesus announced his ministry in the prophetic terms of proclaiming "good news to the poor . . . [and] release to the captives" (Luke 4:16-19), and he challenged the seats of power and exploitation as he ran the moneychangers out of the Temple (Matthew 21:12-16; Mark 11:15-18; Luke 19:45-48; John 2:13-16).

The *theology of hope* finds grounding in the Scripture's emphasis on *eschatology*, the end things or last things. Jesus' teaching about the kingdom or reign of God clearly saw it as a present reality and a future hope. Disciples are warned to watch for signs of the Kingdom's coming (Matthew 24:42-44; Mark 13:4-37; Luke 12:35-40). The resurrection of Christ is seen as inaugurating the reign of Christ over sin and death, and the Book of Revelation calls for faithfulness in anticipation of God's new heaven and new earth. Paul calls the church to take hope in the Resurrection and the coming of the Lord (1 Thessalonians 4:13-18) and to live as children of a new age (Ephesians 3:19-22; Colossians 1:15-20).

Feminist theology's challenge to the masculine bias of Christian theology finds roots in Scripture's multiple images for God and in its inclusive message of equality before God. Genesis 1:27 affirms that women and men possess the image of God. And Paul proclaims, "There is no longer male and female; for all of you are one in Christ Jesus" (Galatians 3:28). Although the Bible reflects the images of a patriarchal society, its basic message supports the full personhood of women and the shattering of masculine idols for the transcendent God who is neither male nor female.

CURRENT THEOLOGICAL DEVELOPMENTS
(*Discipline*, ¶ 104; student book, pages 42–54)

The United Methodist theological statement affirms the significant role played by theologies responding to the unique challenges of the modern world. "We are a Church with a distinctive theological heritage, but that heritage is lived out in a global community, resulting in understandings of our faith enriched by indigenous experiences and manners of expression" (*Discipline*, ¶ 104; student book, page 51).

Many developments in theology have occurred in response to the challenges of the contemporary world. The developments are attempts to discern God's presence and purposes in a time of rapid change and new demands. They are efforts to understand, live, and communicate Christian faith in fresh, relevant categories and images.

It is important to remember that theological explorations are not the same as doctrinal standards. The theological developments considered in this session are theological explorations, not doctrinal standards. They emerge from particular situations, and they attempt to define and apply the faith to issues and needs emerging in a time of rapid change. The various theological developments are, of necessity, tentative and exploratory. Basic doctrine serves as a port from which the explorations are launched and to which they return.

Because United Methodists share commitment to a core of doctrine and agree on basic sources and criteria for theological inquiry, we can consider diverse theological options without losing our center. We also can disagree about theological trends while exhibiting the traditional Wesleyan "catholic spirit": in essentials, unity; in nonessentials, freedom; in all things, clarity.

The following information is a brief summary of four developments in theology. The descriptions are limited to the basic metaphors around which the developments emerge. Think of the four theological approaches described as examples of how theological exploration emerges in response to changing situations.

Process Theology

Ours is a world of rapid change. Science has documented that creation itself is in a perpetual state of flux. Charles Darwin's theory of evolution challenged the image of a static world of fixed species and replaced that image with a picture of a dynamic world of evolving forms of life. Albert Einstein's theory of relativity provided an alternative to Newton's vision of the world as a machine with various parts working in accordance with mechanical laws. Einstein's view is of an interrelated and interdependent world of constant change. Underlying the world of seemingly fixed and separate objects are atoms swirling as energy that connects and shapes reality.

Science reveals a world in which everything is interdependent and contingent. Everything is related to everything else, and no event occurs in a vacuum or in isolation. A sense of transience pervades human experience, as events and societies and persons come into being and pass away. The awareness of contingency and transience is accompanied by a consciousness of relativity. Since everything is contingent and temporary, no entity or experience or achievement can be absolute. Everything is conditioned by its environment and therefore cannot claim to be normative for all environments.

How is God to be understood in a contingent, transient, and relative world? Process theology is a response to that question. Although its various exponents contain many strands and distinctions, process theology generally maintains that what is real is essentially in process.

According to process thought, every enduring entity, including God, can be described in terms of a past, a present, and a future. The past consists of actual experiences that have passed from a momentary "subjective immediacy" into a fixed "objective immortality." That objective past accounts in part for the composition of present, subjective entities. Each entity in the present comes to be as part of a whole society of entities that influence and contribute to its existence. The entity as subject is also shaped by its future possibilities. There is in all existence a lure or pull toward the actualizing of future possibilities.

God is within this whole process as the lure or pull toward the actualization of potential. God is that which integrates the various entities of the universe and lures them with love toward the fulfillment of their potential.

As an integrating and actualizing reality of life, God feels all of life's pain and joy. God experiences the world and is deeply affected by that experience. Because God is always receiving from and responding to all of creation, God is always in the process of becoming. Because every entity receives from and gives to other entities, all of creation is in the process of becoming. God has endowed reality with freedom. God knows all the alternatives for all creatures, but God does not know ahead of time which alternatives will be actualized. The actual outcome depends on the choices exercised by a myriad of entities in response to their given environments and their possible futures.

Creation remains incomplete as chaos and suffering plague humanity and the natural order. Process theology emphasizes the creativity of God in bringing order out of chaos by lovingly luring all of life toward wholeness. As life responds positively and obediently to God's pull toward wholeness, creation is healed and God rejoices.

Theology of Hope

The theology of hope responds to a world preoccupied with the future and the desire to rise above the defeats and failures of the past and present. Theologians of hope contend that hope is the focal metaphor for understanding theology today. They give two reasons. First, hope is a universal structure and process of human existence. Second, theologians of hope contend that hope is the central category of biblical faith.

Jurgen Moltmann roots his theology of hope in two dominant themes in Christian theology—*Christology* (the doctrine of Christ) and *eschatology* (the doctrine of the end or consummation of history). Christ's death and resurrection reveal a reality that runs through all of human history: God will bring life out of death. The Crucifixion affirms God's experience of human suffering, defeat, and death. The Resurrection proclaims God's promise of new life and a transformed future.

Moltmann contends that only a faith in a crucified Christ can withstand the horrors of life's experiences. Only hope inspired by God's promise in the resurrected Christ can appropriate the resurrecting experiences of life. Christ's resurrection is the assurance that God's promise of the future will be fulfilled. How and when that promise will come to completion depend on the response of persons who live in "hopeful faith and faithful hope."

The eschatology of Moltmann and other theologians of hope differs from the traditional image of "the end." Traditional eschatology places God's future at the end of history when God will bring triumph and victory. These theologians counter that God comes into the present from out of the future. God's promise of a new future transforms the present.

God ceases to be a "vertical God" who is either above human existence or within it. God is viewed as a "horizontal God" who connects the future with the present by promise. The hoped-for future comes into the present, but it is always something other than the present. The promises of God result in a new identity; however, the new present identity is only an intimation of the future that is coming toward the present.

Humanity's hope and God's transforming promises are social and political, not individual or otherworldly. God's reign will triumph over all the evils that threaten the world's wholeness. God's promises include a just and peaceful world where poverty, exploitation, and oppression are conquered. Those who live by hope in God's promises throw themselves into efforts to actualize those promises in this world in the here and now while recognizing that any ful-

filled promise is but a foreshadowing of God's inexhaustible future.

Theology of Liberation

Liberation is another significant framework for continuing inquiry into God and God's relationship to the world. A growing consciousness of the oppressive and dehumanizing nature of political, social, economic, and religious structures makes liberation a goal of increasing numbers of the world's people. Liberation movements throughout the world are motivating individuals and groups to use their power to change their environment, their society, and themselves.

Where is God in a world of oppression and revolution? God is the Liberator, the One who stirs and empowers the oppressed toward freedom, according to theologians of liberation.

According to these theologians, the many freedom movements throughout the world challenge Christianity in two ways. On one hand, they confront the church with its racism, sexism, and colonialism. They show that religious beliefs, practices, and structures that identify with the world's advantaged and powerful or disregard the world's powerless are a source of oppression.

On the other hand, liberation theologies confront the church with an opportunity to recover its authentic faith and voice. The God of the Bible is always at work among the marginalized, those without economic, social, and political power. By joining God among the oppressed, the church itself can be liberated from its captivity to prevailing values, practices, and structures.

Liberation theologies differ from the older liberal social gospel movement in that they rise from within disadvantaged peoples, who are uniquely situated to see the world as it really is and as it ought to be. The social gospel of an earlier era consisted predominantly of the advantaged seeking to change the plight of the disadvantaged. "Liberation theologies are theologies *of* the oppressed, *by* the oppressed, and *for* the oppressed."[1]

Liberation theologies ordinarily do not address the problems of oppressed groups *en masse*. Rather, they are written from the perspective of distinctive groups. Ethnic, feminist, and Third World groups address the issues from their own distinct perspectives. They do, however, share some basic affirmations.

Liberation theologies affirm God's solidarity with the oppressed. They also proclaim God's goal of freedom from all forms of oppression. Further, freedom comes to the oppressor as well as to the oppressed when those held in economic, political, social, or sexual bondage are freed. Liberation calls for revolutionary obedience to the liberating God who breaks down all walls that divide persons and works to build new communities of justice and equality.

Feminist Theology

Classifying feminist theology as a separate theological development may be misleading, because women are making significant contributions in all theologies. For example, Marjorie Suchocki is a major voice in process thought; Rosemary Radford Ruether in liberation theologies; and, Sallie McFague in theology as story and metaphor. As a group, however, women theologians bring to theological exploration dimensions and emphases that emerge from their own experiences.

Feminist theology is not to be understood primarily as theological reflection on separate, "feminine" themes. Feminist theology, rather, offers a critique of a patriarchal and masculine bias in traditional theology and explores non-masculine understandings of God. Feminist theology reflects on the negative impact of the masculine bias on women as well as its influence in shaping understandings of God. Feminist theology reflects on the negative impact of the masculine bias on women as well as its influence in shaping understandings of God, nature, sin, grace, Christology, redemption, and the church.

The reevaluation of Christian symbols in terms of feminist experience results in rethinking the concept of God as a hierarchical being who seeks domination and control through authoritarian relationships. Rather, God is seen as one who in travail gives birth and nurtures creation toward wholeness, as a mother gives birth to a child and nurtures the child to maturity. God is pictured in the metaphors of mother, lover, and friend.

As models of God change, so do models of the world and God's relationship to it. Rather than the world being viewed as a detached creation of God, it can be seen as God's body, which is nurtured, sustained, and preserved in its magnificent splendor and mystery. Such a model of God has enormous relevance in our nuclear age.[2]

Feminist theology also questions the traditional understanding of such Christian concepts as sin and grace. "When, for example, sin is seen primarily in terms of overweening pride and grace as redeeming humility, one has a theological pattern of men in power," writes Rosemary Radford Ruether. Such an understanding of sin and redemption "may be much less relevant to women or oppressed people, whose sin has been more the failure to affirm the self."[3] For such persons, "humility" may be understood as acquiesce to unjust authority or subjugation to oppressive power.

Feminist theology derives from the experience of women and seeks to interpret the Christian faith in light of that experience. Its challenge to the male bias in traditional theology and in much of institutional religion pushes the church to explore additional models of God, the world, personhood, sin, and redemption. Feminist theology argues that models other than the traditional ones are appropriate and illuminating for expressing the Christian gospel in our time and that those models prompt Christians to admit "God has many names."[4]

Conclusion

Theological exploration is an inevitable and necessary component of faith if we are to make disciples of Jesus Christ. The Bible itself contains the story of people exploring their understanding of God and relationship to God in the context of social, cultural, and personal realities. Explorations grow out of the inadequacy of doctrines to comprehend God fully, and they emerge as attempts to interpret the doctrines in light of emerging realities.

Current developments in theology, therefore, can claim a long tradition. They are not to be seen as doctrines that compete with the core faith of the church. Rather, they are theological inquiries and explorations that are to be judged by their faithfulness to doctrine and to the God who transcends formulations.

Many theological developments merit attention and study by United Methodists. In addition to more detailed study of the four kinds of theology briefly described in this session, the following are among many options that offer helpful insights: metaphorical theology, narrative theology, evangelical theology, and theologies of play. With a firm grounding in our doctrinal roots, sources, and guidelines, United Methodists can continue theological exploration with courage, creativity, and hope.

THE SESSION PLAN

Have available in the classroom books and articles that illustrate the diversity of recent developments in theology. Books listed for this session in "For Further Study" (pages 113–14 in this leader's guide) should be among those available. Have written on pieces of construction paper and posted on the walls various words and phrases such as the following: *Process Theology, Theology of Hope, Liberation Theology, Feminist Theology, Theologies of Play, Evangelical Theology, God as Process, the World as God's Body, God as the Mind of the Universe, God as Liberator.* Also display prominently the mobile of the four sources and criteria for theological inquiry from Session 10.

1. Begin the session with a statement similar to the following: "Many voices are being heard in theology today. Some are soft voices; others are strident. Some come from peoples of other tongues and cultures; others emerge from within our own borders. All the voices represent challenging attempts to explore the meaning of God and God's relationship to the contemporary world. Because we as United Methodists stand on a foundation of doctrine and possess valid sources and criteria for doing theology, we can listen to the voices. Within them we may discern the voice of God and be better able to be in ministry in the modern world. We may also find meaningful ways by which our own voice can be added to those who seek to discern and live God's message in a changing world."

2. Make clear the distinction between doctrinal standards and theological exploration. Doctrinal standards represent the foundation upon which additional structures are built. Doctrines are statements of faith that the church affirms. Theological exploration is the interpretation, expansion, and reflection on doctrines in light of contemporary realities. Theological exploration remains open to new directions of thought and perception. In this session, we are dealing with theological exploration.

3. Divide the class into four teams: one team each for process theology, liberation theology, the theology of hope, and feminist theology. Read aloud or distribute copies of the cases of John and Susan from Session 10. Also summarize the information about the four theologies in this leader's guide and give the information to teams. In addition, call attention to the books and articles you have available. Have each team read the summary of its respective theology. Have teams review the cases of John and Susan in terms of the theology assigned to them. Write on chalkboard or posterboard the following questions each team should address:
1. How would _____ [process theology, theology of hope, theology of liberation, feminist theology] respond to John's assumption that God controls all events?
2. What would _____ have to say about the cause of John's suffering?
3. How would _____ respond to the prayer group's statement to Karen: "God can do all things"?
4. What about John's statement: "Or maybe God is just a weak God who can't do anything about things like cancer"?
5. How would _____ fit in with the pastor's statement that God's power is the power of love?
6. What would _____ have to say to Susan's assumption that she needs to believe all the Bible and all the church says in order to be a Christian?
7. Does _____ allow for belief in evolution?
8. How would _____ be able to help Susan deal with her doubts?

Circulate among the teams as they work. If possible, enlist the pastor or another person who may have some familiarity with the various theologies to be present and available as a resource person.

After allowing enough time for the teams to respond to the questions, ask each team to report briefly to the class. The report should include the origin of the particular theology, its basic or principal emphasis, and its major contribution to John and Susan.

4. Choose an issue identified in Session 11, such as the challenge of modern science, the world as a global village filled with suffering people, the vastness of space and the impersonal nature of modern life. Ask team members to consider the issue in terms of their designated theology. What implications do process, liberation, hope, and feminist theologies have for the issue? (For example, process theology would see creation as ongoing and incomplete. It interprets God as personal in new ways. All the theologies identify God as working within the events and realities of the contemporary world.)

5. Raise this question: How do these developments in theology fare according to the guidelines of Scripture, tradition, reason, and experience? Although time does not allow for full discussion of the question in this session, remind group members that such evaluation is necessary. Group members might begin by applying one or two guidelines to one kind of theology as fully as time allows.

6. Ask the groups representing the various theologies to respond to this question: What insights does your theology (process, liberation, hope, feminist) provide to the church for fulfilling its mission "to make disciples of Jesus Christ"? How do they inform our understanding and practice of ministry as described in the *Discipline*, ¶¶ 126–37; student book, pages 57–61?

7. Summarize the session with a statement similar to the following: "Just as the Bible contains both doctrine and theological exploration, The United Methodist Church continues to listen with discernment to the diverse voices in the contemporary theological chorus. Knowing that new demands teach new duties and that God is forever making all things new, we remain open to fresh insights and untraveled pathways. As we explore, we remain grounded in our doctrinal standards; and we explore with the tools of Scripture, tradition, reason, and experience."

8. Close by singing or reading the hymn "God of Many Names" (*The United Methodist Hymnal*, Number 105).

---

[1] From *The Shattered Spectrum: A Survey of Contemporary Theology*, by Lonnie D. Kliever (John Knox Press, 1981), page 75.
[2] See *Models of God*, by Sallie McFague (Fortress Press, 1987), pages 69–78.
[3] From "Feminist Theology," by Rosemary Radford Ruether, in *The Westminster Dictionary of Christian Theology*, edited by Alan Richardson and John Bowden (The Westminster Press, 1983), pages 211–12.
[4] From *Models of God*, page 182.

OUR ECUMENICAL COMMITMENT

Purpose of This Session:

To help adults see that ecumenical dialogue and missional cooperation between United Methodists and other Christians is a valid witness to the unity of the body of Christ and that all Christians, as both neighbors and witnesses to persons of other faiths, can and should welcome interfaith conversations and cooperation.

Goals of This Session:

1. To help study group members understand that cooperation with other Christians is in line with the biblical image of the church and an indispensable part of our Wesleyan heritage.
2. To motivate adults to learn about other world religions and to enter into dialogue with persons of other faiths.
3. To challenge participants to seek ways by which their local church can reflect more fully the unity among Christians.

GROUNDING IN SCRIPTURE

The Bible bears witness to both the particularity and universality of God's purpose and activity. On one hand, God entered into a covenant with Abraham and promised to make of his descendants a great nation (Genesis 12:1-2). God delivered the Hebrew slaves from bondage in Egypt and led them to become a nation (Exodus). They were to be God's own people.

On the other hand, God's purposes and activity are not limited to the nation of Israel. Abraham was called to be the father of a nation, but the nation was to be a means by which "all the families of the earth shall be blessed" (Genesis 12:3). The prophets clearly affirmed God's particular covenant with Israel while at the same time acknowledging God's sovereignty over all nations. Amos declared to the people of Israel:

"You only have I known
   of all the families of the earth" (Amos 3:2).
But he also said,
"Are you not like the Ethiopians to me,
   O people of Israel? says the LORD.
Did I not bring Israel up from the land
   of Egypt,
   and the Philistines from Caphtor and
   the Arameans from Kir?" (9:7).

The Book of Jonah is a warning to those who would limit God's salvation and love to a particular people. God's call is clearly for the purpose of responsibility rather than privilege. Jonah was confronted with God's universal mercy, extending even to Israel's enemies. And it was Jonah's responsibility to be a means by which the divine mercy was known.

God's particular call, then, is cause for humility and faithfulness, not for arrogance and presumption. Though Israel was called to be "the people of God," the nation had no monopoly on God's love or presence. God frequently came to the chosen people through persons who did not even acknowledge God's existence. For example, Cyrus, the king of Persia, who defeated Babylon and permitted the exiles to return to their homeland is referred to as God's "anointed" (Isaiah 45:1).

The Old Testament affirms both the particular expression of God's purposes and love in a chosen community *and* God's universal sovereignty and love for all peoples. God chooses peoples, not to promote exclusiveness, but as a means of blessing all peoples.

The particularity and universality of God's sovereignty, love, and purposes come together in Jesus Christ. God acts in a special way in Jesus Christ to bring all humanity into harmony with God and one another (John 3:16; 2 Corinthians 5:19-20; Galatians 3:28-29). Jesus refused to limit God's presence and activity to those who shared his beliefs about God. He commended a Roman soldier for his faith (Luke 7:9). He rebuked the disciples for stopping a nondisciple from casting out demons (Mark 9:38-40). And he made a Samaritan the hero of one of his most memorable stories (Luke 10:29-37). Jesus' "priestly prayer" in John's Gospel affirms the oneness of the church. Jesus prayed, "I ask not only on behalf of these, but also on behalf of those who will believe in me through their word, that they may all be one. As you, Father, are in me and I am in you, may they also be in us, so that the world may believe that you have sent me" (John 17:20-21). Only through unity can the church reflect the reality of God in the world and effectively bear witness to the reconciling love of Christ.

A conflict in the first century focused on the relationship between the church and Judaism. Were God's redemptive acts in Jesus Christ limited to the Jews? Was the church to include Jews and Gentiles? Paul argued for the inclusiveness of God's promises (Acts 15:6-21; Romans 11:13-36; Galatians 2:6-21).

Peter's vision and later encounter with the Gentile Cornelius led him reluctantly to the conclusion that "God shows no partiality, but in every nation anyone who fears him and does what is right is acceptable to him" (Acts 10:34).

The dominant images of the church in the New Testament are described in Session 1. Those images affirm the oneness and essential unity of the church amid its diversity and variety of gifts. As previous sessions have indicated, no one denomination is the body of Christ. All Christian communions function together, as organs of the body function cooperatively and with mutual dependency.

To be true to the biblical witness and to the very nature of God, The United Methodist Church seeks to cooperate with other denominations, advocating full reception of the gift of Christian unity, and to converse with other religions. Only through such efforts will Christ's prayer "that they may all be one" be answered.

WHAT THE *DISCIPLINE* SAYS
(*Discipline*, ¶¶ 104, 120–131, 138; student book, pages 42–54, 55–59, 61)

"Christian unity is founded on the theological understanding that through faith in Jesus Christ we are made members-in-common of the one body of Christ. Christian unity is not an option; it is a gift to be received and expressed" (*Discipline*, ¶ 104; student book, page 52).

United Methodism began as a movement within the Church of England. John Wesley did not intend to create another denomination. He saw "the people called Methodists" as existing to reform the church and the nation. He was reluctant to put into motion the necessary forces, particularly the origination of clergy, to form the new church in America. He considered himself an Anglican to the end of his life.

Wesley's Ecumenical Spirit

The historic ecumenical spirit of The United Methodist Church finds support in Wesley's own "catholic spirit." In a sermon entitled "A Caution against Bigotry," Wesley confronted the tendency of Methodists and non-Methodists to resist the activity of God when it was done under auspices other than their own. His text was Mark 9:38-39: "John said to him, 'Teacher, we saw someone casting out demons in your name, and we tried to stop him, because he was not following us.' But Jesus said, 'Do not stop him.' " The following is an excerpt from Wesley's sermon:

Am I not convicted of bigotry in this, in forbidding him . . . on this ground, because he is not of my *party*? Because he does not fall in with my *opinions*? Or because he does not worship God according to that scheme of religion which I have received from my fathers? . . .

. . . What if I were to see a Papist, an

Arian, a Socinian casting out devils? If I did, I could not forbid even him without convicting myself of bigotry. Yea, if it could be supposed that I should see a Jew, a deist, or a Turk doing the same, were I to forbid him either directly or indirectly I should be no better than a bigot still. . . .

. . . Encourage whomsoever God is pleased to employ, to give himself wholly up thereto. Speak well of him wheresoever you are; defend his character and his mission. Enlarge as far as you can his sphere of action. Show him all kindness in word and deed.[1]

Wesley's nondogmatic method in theology and his inclusive view of the church are forcefully proclaimed in his sermon, "Catholic Spirit." Wesley wrote:

I dare not therefore presume to impose my mode of worship on any other. I believe it is truly primitive and apostolical. But my belief is no rule for another. I ask not therefore of him with whom I would unite in love, "Are you of my Church? Of my congregation? Do you receive the same form of church government and allow the same church officers with me? Do you join in the same form of prayer wherein I worship God?" I inquire not, "Do you receive the Supper of the Lord in the same posture and manner that I do?" Nor, whether, in the administration of baptism, you agree with me in admitting sureties for the baptized, in the manner of administering it, or the age of those to whom it should be admonished. . . . Let all these things stand by; we will talk of them, if need be, at a more convenient season. My only question at present is this, "Is thine heart right, as my heart is with thy heart?"[2]

The sermon proceeds to spell out Wesley's convictions that love for God and neighbor is the heart of religion and the catholic (universal) spirit is catholic (universal) love.

Wesley affirmed the importance of faithfulness to the core doctrines of the faith, but he believed that beyond the divisions separating Christians into denominations was a transcending love that bound them together. In a letter to Mrs. Howton, October 3, 1783, he wrote: " 'It is the glory of the people called Methodists that they condemn none for the opinions or modes of worship. They think and let think.' He had laid down the same principle, much earlier, in *The Character of a Methodist* (1742) . . . : 'As to all opinions which do not strike at the root of Christianity, we 'think and let think.' "[3] The principle runs through Wesley's life and works: In essentials, unity; in nonessentials, freedom; in all things, charity.

The catholic spirit appreciates and affirms diversity while holding strong beliefs. Wesley held both strong convictions and strong opinions, yet he felt no compulsion to require that others conform to his ideas. Conforming to the image of Christ, becoming perfect in love, was his goal and the goal he sought for all persons. For Wesley, failure to love another because of the other's religious beliefs or practices was the very negation of religion.

Tolerance, however, is not to be equated with indifference. Genuine tolerance involves taking differences seriously, while indifference ignores the differences. Tolerance includes understanding the beliefs, perceptions, and practices of those with whom one differs and being willing to listen to the others' points of view. Tolerance acknowledges that all perceptions of God are limited; therefore, humility and openness to diversity are required if one is to know God.

For Wesley and for United Methodists today, beliefs and doctrines are subordinate to love. We refuse to discard the heart of religion, love for God and neighbor, in arguments over religion.

Necessity of Unity Among Christians

The nature of God, the spirit of Christ, and the mission of the church require unity and cooperation among Christians.

Since God is the one sovereign of all creation and since the church is called to reflect the image of God, the church has no choice but to strive for oneness. A dominant biblical image of God's vision for the world is that the human family will be one, that people will come to know themselves as brothers and sisters under the parenthood of God. The church is summoned toward that vision. It is to be an outpost of God's dream for the whole world.

Unity in the Godhead, however, includes diversity. Diversity within unity is at the very core of reality. Creation itself is made up of a countless variety of species, yet all are united in a delicate ecological system. The church that seeks mere homogeneity, everybody like everybody else, runs contrary to the nature of God and the character of reality.

It is in diversity that we come to know the fullness of God's grace. Dialogue, in an atmosphere of mutual respect and love, results in broader understanding and deepened love. As the theological statement says, "In these encounters, our aim is not to reduce doctrinal differences to some lowest common denominator of religious agreement, but to raise all such relationships to the highest possible level of human fellowship and understanding" (*Discipline*, ¶ 104; student book, page 53).

Further, unity among Christians is imperative if the church is to bear witness in today's world. If churches cannot cooperate in mutual respect and mission, the church has little to offer a divided and hostile world. If Christians cannot learn to love and work with one another, their witness on behalf of God's *shalom,* God's peace, is made null and void.

The needs facing the world require a sharing of resources by the Christian church. In a world of mass starvation, rampant disease, growing illiteracy, serious environmental threats, epidemic addictions, and threatened annihilation from war, churches can ill afford competitiveness and duplication or fragmentation of efforts. Cooperation is required at all levels, from churches in local communities to broader denominational and ecumenical agencies.

The *Discipline* (¶ 129; student book, page 58) declares: "There is but one ministry in Christ." As part of the church universal, we join with other Christians in ministry to the world as a sharing in Christ's ministry. Sharing resources and gifts with other disciples of Jesus Christ as we reach out in ministry to the world is one means of modeling the self-giving love of God. Participation in mutual ministries is also one way to foster dialogue and overcome the separation among members of Christ's body.

Dialogue With Other World Religions

Recent world events have highlighted the need for better understanding among the world's great religions. In the world's global village, diverse religions play critical roles among its people. Many of the violent conflicts that threaten the peace of the global village are motivated and fueled by religion. Peace will require religious dialogue as well as political dialogue.

What is The United Methodist Church's response to other religions? The theological statement says, "As people bound together on one planet, we see the need for a self-critical view of our own tradition and accurate appreciation of other traditions" (*Discipline*, ¶ 104; student book, page 53). The statement affirms dialogue with other religions and calls us "to reflect anew on our faith and to seek guidance for our witness among neighbors of other faiths. We then rediscover that the God who has acted in Jesus Christ for the salvation of the whole world is also the Creator of all humankind, the One who is 'above all and through all and in all' (Ephesians 4:6)" (*Discipline*, ¶ 104; student book, page 53).

Creative interaction with other religions requires that Christians evaluate their concepts of evangelism and mission. Tough questions must be raised: Is God's goal to make the world "Christian"? Is it possible for persons to experience the reality of Christ in other religions? Is there a difference between winning converts to the Christian church and winning persons to Christ-likeness? If God is one and the sovereign of all peoples, do different peoples experience God's presence and redemptive activity but refer to the experience in different language and symbols? Is it possible that some Christians may be more concerned about converting people to their own symbols and rituals than enabling persons to experience the One whose very nature and name is love?

As we have seen, the biblical story emphasizes that God's activity and purposes cannot be confined to one nation or one religion. God's blessing of Ishmael, for example, as the progenitor of a people alongside the Jews (Genesis 16:1-12; 21:8-21), testifies to the inclusiveness of God's activity. Amos's affirmation that other nations besides Israel were also chosen and led by God serves as a warning to those who would limit God's actions to their nation or religion (Amos 9:7).

Dialogue is a legitimate form of exchange of witness in the contemporary pluralistic world. It too has roots in Scripture. Paul confronted persons of diverse philosophies, cultures, and religions when he went to Athens. His approach to the Athenians, though unsuccessful at the time, provides a model for one form of evangelism. Paul, familiar with Greek philosophy and the pluralistic Athenian culture, acknowledged the people's quest. He quoted from a Greek philosopher to describe his concept of God: "In him we live and move and have our being" (Acts 17:28). He said, "What therefore you worship as unknown, this I proclaim to you" (17:23). He understood and appreciated their experiences and insights and sought to expand and give new meaning to their images and concepts.

Evangelism in today's world requires that we take seriously the experiences, insights, and images of other cultures and religions. Religious imperialism today is as ineffective as the colonialism of a former era. We do not take Christ to others. We find Christ in others. The risen One comes among us as we share with others in a mutual quest for the God who knows no boundaries and who cannot be contained in any religion.

Conclusion

The nature and mission of the church and our United Methodist heritage require an ecumenical perspective. Learning to live with and appreciate diversity enables the church to model the meaning of community. As God's own essence includes unity amid diversity, the church must resist efforts to reduce congregations and denominations to homogeneous fellowships. Instead, the church must seek to reflect God's vision for the human family.

Our proper role in interfaith dialogue is not to disparage other great religions of the world. Rather, we should speak and live as witnesses to the truth made known to us in Jesus Christ.

THE SESSION PLAN

Note to the leader:

Since this is the last session of the study, you will need to reflect on the previous class sessions and be prepared to tie up loose ends; however, the major portion of time should be spent on "Our Ecumenical Commitment." My sense is that most local churches do not consider the topic of vital interest and concern. You will need to be creative in involving participants in the issue.

1. Assign one or more class members the responsibility to read and report on the two sermons by John Wesley quoted in this leader's guide: "A Caution against Bigotry" and "Catholic Spirit." Put relevant quotations on posterboard and display them around the room. In addition to the quotations in this leader's guide, you might include the following:
- "Think not the bigotry of another is any excuse for your own" (from "A Caution against Bigotry").[4]
- "Every wise man therefore will allow others the same liberty of thinking which he desires they should allow him; and will no more insist on their embracing his opinions than he would have them to insist on his embracing theirs" (from "Catholic Spirit").[5]
- "Observe this, you who know not what spirit ye are of, who call yourselves men of a catholic spirit only because you are of a muddy understanding; because your mind is all in a mist; because you have no settled, consistent principles, but are for jumbling all opinions together" (from "Catholic Spirit").[6]
- "A man of a catholic spirit is one who . . . 'gives his hand' to all whose 'hearts are right with his heart' " (from "Catholic Spirit").[7]

After hearing the reports or studying the quotations, ask this question: What are the implications of Wesley's sermons for our church's relationship with other churches in our community? Allow time for responses and discussion.

2. For this step, each individual or team of individuals will need a Bible. If possible, have a variety of translations available.

On separate index cards, write all four of these statements:
1. God is partial to Christians.
2. God blesses only those who believe correctly about God.
3. Only Christians are saved.
4. God chooses particular people or churches in order to accomplish a broader purpose for all humankind.

On the other side of all the cards, write these biblical references: Genesis 12:2-3; Amos 9:7; Matthew 7:21; Luke 13:29-30; John 10:16; 14:6; 17:20-21; Acts 4:12; 10:34. Distribute the cards to individual class members or to teams of individuals (depending on the size of the class). Ask the individuals or teams to answer "true" or "false" to the statements *before* looking up the Scripture references on the reverse side. Allow time for everyone to locate and read the Bible passages. Then invite participants to answer the true or false questions again.

Bring the class together. Ask these questions: Which comments are true? Which are false? Which answers did you change after you read the Scripture?

Participants probably will not agree on all the answers. The longer the discussion, the more obvious that a simple "true" or "false" is an inadequate answer to any of these questions. The class discussion, however, should make these points: (1) God's purposes extend to all persons. (2) God chooses particular persons or churches, not for privilege, but as a means of blessing others. (3) Diversity of interpretation exists even among class members, and yet the class remains one.

3. Report to the class that Carl Sandburg was once asked by an interviewer, What is the ugliest world in the English language? After what seemed to be an excessive time of reflection, Sandburg responded, "Exclusive." Ask your group members these questions: According to the biblical material and Wesley's sermons that you have read in this session, do you think Sandburg was correct? Religion often appeals to the desire to be exclusive, special, among the elect. Which more accurately describes God's

relationship to the world—*exclusive* or *inclusive*? Give illustrations from the passages discussed in the previous two activities.

4. The relationship between the church and other religions is an area in which additional theological inquiry and exploration are needed. Using the criteria of Scripture, tradition, experience, and reason, have the class evaluate the material in this leader's guide under the heading "Dialogue With Other World Religions." This activity could be time-consuming and difficult for the entire class, but perhaps a member would be interested in taking it on as a challenge.

OR

4. One way to give life to the session would be to invite representatives of other denominations and other religions to the class—perhaps a Roman Catholic priest, a Jewish rabbi, a Protestant clergyperson, a Muslim, and a Hindu. Have them form a panel to discuss the following questions, which you would need to give to them in advance: How does your religion view other religions? What suggestions do you have for promoting understanding and cooperation among the world's religions? In what ministries globally and locally does your religion participate with other faith groups?

Allow opportunity for questions and comments from the class. Also, an informal time before or after the class session would enable class members and guests to get to know one another as persons.

5. Divide the class into two teams. Have one team read Matthew 5:13-16 and then list the qualities of salt and light. Ask members of the first team to discuss among themselves the implications of the qualities of light and salt for our role as witnesses in the world. Ask the other team to read Acts 17:16-31 and list the methods used by Paul in witnessing to the Athenians. Have members of the second team discuss the implications of Paul's approach for how we might relate to persons outside the Christian faith. Then have both teams report the results of their discussions to the total class.

6. Invite class members to list ways your local

church is working with other denominations and other religions. The list could include efforts such as the following: community ecumenical worship services on special occasions, sharing in a food pantry or clothing distribution center, financial support of ecumenical ministries, use of the ecumenical lectionary, mission and Advance Special projects that are ecumenical agencies, American Bible Society, and so forth.

7. The theological task of The United Methodist Church remains unfinished. The present theological statement in the *Discipline* is subject to change by General Conference. Encourage class members to petition General Conference if they feel that changes are warranted. For the petition to receive adequate attention, it should identify the specific change requested and the rationale for the change. You may even want to write a petition as a study group and bring it before the Administrative Council or Council on Ministries in your local church.

8. Close the session with prayers from class members with each petition being followed by the response "Hear our prayer, O God."

Or you may prefer to close with this benediction, which is the conclusion of the theological statement:

"Now to God
who by the power at work within us
is able to do far more abundantly
than all that we ask or think,
to God be glory in the church
and in Christ Jesus to all generations,
for ever and ever. Amen.
—Ephesians 3:20-21 (based on RSV)"
(*Discipline*, ¶ 104; student book, page 54).

---

[1] From *The Works of John Wesley, Volume 2*, edited by Albert C. Outler (Abingdon Press, 1985), page 77.

[2] From *The Works of John Wesley, Volume 2*, pages 86–87.

[3] From *The Works of John Wesley, Volume 1*, edited by Albert C. Outler (Abingdon Press, 1984), page 87.

[4] From *The Works of John Wesley, Volume 2*, page 78.

[5] From *The Works of John Wesley, Volume 2*, page 84.

[6] From *The Works of John Wesley, Volume 2*, page 93.

[7] From *The Works of John Wesley, Volume 2*, page 94.

FOR FURTHER STUDY

Session 1

Images of the Church in the New Testament, by Paul S. Minear (The Westminster Press, 1960). A classic study of ninety-six New Testament images of the church.

The Church Confident, by Leander Keck (Abingdon Press, 1993). A concise, clear call to renewal in the context of contemporary challenges to the church.

Polity, Practice, and the Mission of The United Methodist Church, by Thomas Edward Frank (Abingdon Press, 1997). A comprehensive treatment of the polity, structure, mission, and practice of The United Methodist Church.

Session 2

The Spirit of Protestantism, by Robert McAfee Brown (Oxford University Press, 1966). A highly readable introduction to basic Protestant affirmations.

Loyalty to God, The Apostles' Creed in Life and Liturgy (Abingdon Press, 1992). A helpful commentary on the Apostles' Creed and the role of creeds in daily living.

Session 3

Introduction to Theology, by Marianne H. Micks (Seabury Press, 1964; revised, Harper and Row, 1983). A good introduction for laity, organized in terms of three categories—Bible, tradition, and reason.

Session 4

The History of the Evangelical United Brethren Church, J. Bruce Behney and Paul H. Eller, edited by Kenneth W. Krueger (Abingdon Press, 1979). A comprehensive study of two historical strands: the Evangelical movement led by Jacob Albright and the United Brethren led by Philip William Otterbein.

Wesley and the People Called Methodists, by Richard P. Heitzenrater (Abingdon Press, 1994). An excellent survey of the Wesleyan movement in the eighteenth century.

Session 5

Responsible Grace, by Randy L. Maddox (Abingdon Press, 1994). A perceptive and comprehensive treatment of Wesleyan theology of grace.

Theology and Evangelism in the Wesleyan Heritage, edited by James C. Logan (Kingswood Books, 1994). A collection of essays by United Methodist scholars and leaders.

The Amnesty of Grace, by Elsa Tamez (Abingdon Press, 1993). A provocative treatment of the corporate dimension of justification of grace.

Session 6

John Wesley's Experimental Divinity: Studies in Methodist Doctrinal Standards, by Robert E. Cushman (Kingswood Books, 1989). Helpful essays by a distinguished Wesley scholar.

The Scripture Way of Salvation, The Heart of John Wesley's Theology, by Kenneth J. Collins (Abingdon Press, 1997). A helpful treatment of the central theme of Wesleyan theology.

Session 7

Principles of Biomedical Ethics, by Tom L. Beauchamp and James F. Childress (Oxford University Press, 1979). See Chapter 4 on the principle of nonmaleficence and Chapter 5 on the principle of beneficence.

Living Our Beliefs, The United Methodist Way, by Kenneth L. Carder (Discipleship Resources, 1996). An overview of United Methodist beliefs and their implications for living.

Session 8

The Nature of Doctrine: Religion and Theology in a Postliberal Age, by George A. Lindbeck (The Westminster Press, 1984). Written for a scholarly audience, this book has generated much discussion in academic and church circles.

Doctrine and Theology in The United Methodist Church, edited by Thomas A. Langford (Kingswood Books, 1991; paper 2001). An excellent collection of essays that set in historical context the official United Methodist theological statements.

Session 9

The Works of John Wesley, four volumes of sermons, edited by Albert C. Outler (Abingdon Press, 1988). The comprehensive source books of Wesley's sermons with helpful introductions and notes by a Wesley scholar.

Wesley and the Quadrilateral, edited by W. Stephen Gunter (Abingdon Press, 1997). A timely analysis of the role of Scripture, tradition, experience, and reason in Wesleyan theology.

Session 10

Not Every Spirit: A Dogmatics of Christian Disbelief, by Christopher Morse (Trinity Press International, 1994). This outstanding introduction to theology creatively illuminates many contemporary issues.

The Will of God, by Leslie Weatherhead (Abingdon Press, 1994; paper 1999). Available as study resource with a workbook. In this perennial best-seller, the last pastor of London's City Temple explores God's intentional will, God's circumstantial will, God's ultimate will, and discerning the will of God.

Narratives of a Vulnerable God, by William C. Placher (Westminster John Knox Press, 1994). The author helps us understand God as a vulnerable, suffering God who meets us in our vulnerability and suffering.

Session 11

EarthCurrents, by Howard A. Snyder (Abingdon Press, 1995). A theological exploration of issues confronting the world.

Your God Is Too Small, by J. B. Phillips (The MacMillan Company, 1952; paper 1987). This popular volume demolishes more than a dozen false images of God.

Session 12

God-Christ-Church: A Practical Guide to Process Theology, by Marjorie Hewitt Suchocki (Crossroad, revised 1990). Explores the deeper existential meaning of process thought in a readable, even eloquent, style.

Models of God: Theology for an Ecological, Nuclear Age, Sallie McFague (Fortress Press, 1989). Explores the importance in our day of four metaphors for God's relationship to the world.

Sexism and God-Talk: Toward a Feminist Theology, Rosemary Radford Ruether (Beacon Pres, 1993). A wide-ranging study by a prominent feminist theologian.

Theology of Hope, by Jurgen Moltmann, translated by James W. Leitch (Fortress Press, 1993). The English translation of the book that launched the theology of hope as a major alternative.

Session 13

Baptism, Eucharist and Ministry 1982–1990 (Faith and Order Paper Number 11, World Council of Churches, 1990). The most widely discussed ecumenical document on the contemporary scene.

Why It Matters: A Popular Introduction to the Baptism, Eucharist, and Ministry Text, by Michael Kinnamon (World Council of Churches, 1985).

CPSIA information can be obtained
at www.ICGtesting.com
Printed in the USA
LVOW01s0238270516

489994LV00011B/36/P

9 781426 778872